Leaderocity™

Leaderocity™

Leading at the Speed of Now

Richard Dool, DMgt.

Co-authors

Tahsin Alam

Zhongyao Cai

Keisha Dabrowski

Stephanie Dresher

Adam C. Gray

Saumil Joshi

Weijia Mao

Ngwa Numfor

Lloyd N. Pearson

Wendy Silverman

Natalie Spangenberg

Hanin Sukayri

Peinong Tan

Alcillena Wilson-Matteis

Alissa J. Zarro

ili BEP

BUSINESS EXPERT PRESS

Leader in applied, concise business books

First published in 2021 by
Business Expert Press, LLC
222 East 46th Street, New York, NY 10017
www.businessexpertpress.com

ISBN-13: 978-1-63742-356-1
ISBN-13: 978-1-95334-937-8 (e-book)

Business Expert Press Human Resource Management and Organizational
Behavior Collection

Collection ISSN: 1946-5637 (print)
Collection ISSN: 1946-5645 (electronic)

Cover image licensed by Ingram Image, StockPhotoSecrets.com
Chapter Icons by: Ngwa Numfor
Cover and interior design by S4Carlisle Publishing Services Private Ltd.,
Chennai, India

10 9 8 7 6 5 4 3 2 1

LEADER⬚CITY™

"Technology, globalization, and the accelerating pace of change have yielded chaotic markets, fierce competition, and unpredictable staff requirements."

— Bruce Tulgan —

Dedication

We hope this book adds to the body of leadership literature in a manner that enables today's leaders or aspiring leaders to use our thoughts on the competencies needed to lead effectively in this century to enhance their brand and practices.

Leaders need to be lifelong learners to stay current or to even get ahead. Leadership has been studied for over a hundred years in the United States and remains a dynamic, ever-shifting field. Our book is intended to offer a set of competencies that leaders can reflect on and potentially deploy. There is no magic formula, leadership is often both contextual and situational. The best leaders deploy their competencies in a tailored manner leveraging their strengths and complementing their lesser skills.

We offer our set of 10 competencies to be considered based on our research, experiences, and more than 30 interviews with current leaders.

It is not meant to be prescriptive, more for consideration by each leader to assess and reflect on their own leadership values, brand, and practices and to decide if what we offer in this book can add to them. We hope both current and aspiring leaders consider our selected competencies and put them into action in a manner that is tailored, personal, and authentic.

To this end we include in each chapter our definition and rationale for each competency as well as what others are saying about it – academics and professionals. We also include trends and situations that demand each competency, as well as suggestions on how to assess, develop, and enhance each competency.

Abstract

This book explores the intersections between leadership and velocity (the speed of now) to identify key leadership competencies needed for the 21st Century. We offer a set of ten competencies that may serve as a foundation of effective leadership that emerged from our experiences, interviews with 30 leaders and research. These competencies may be especially timely in the midst of the global COVID-19 crisis and the need for effective leadership at all levels. We can see both the critical need for these competencies as well as the stark contrasts in practice – those leaders who are rising to the moment and others whose lacking is disappointingly notable. We hope this book may enable leaders to establish their leadership brand and enhance their leadership practices.

Keywords

Leadership, management, vision, purpose, exemplar, talent manager, change agent, producer, coach, mentor, diversity, multicultural, connector, advocate, ambassador, inclusion, exemplar, producer, talent manager, leadership competencies

Contents

Introduction

This book had its genesis in my time as an executive with General Electric, the company that has long been acclaimed for its leadership development. Venerable behemoths like GE, IBM, P&G, and McKinsey have historically been viewed as CEO factories; indeed, 20.5 percent of all CEOs appointed at the S&P 1500 firms from 1992 to 2010 came from 36 CEO factories such as these, with GE being the largest (Botelho and Kos, 2020). GE's famed Crotonville Learning Center in NY has been developing GE leaders since the 1950s. Twelve thousand employees are trained each year in an array of leadership development programs. CEO magazine named GE one of the "Best Companies for Leadership" in 2016.

GE recognized that some of its leadership development content and activities were dated and needed a significant refresh to meet the global demands that GE was facing. A GE executive noted: "A key Crotonville focus, says GE's Leimonitis, is around what 21st-century leadership looks like, at a time of such disruption and when multiple generations are entering the workforce" (Nicholls, 2017).

GE conducted a multiyear study to update and refresh the leadership competencies needed to be effective in this century. GE's chief learning officer, Raghu Krishnamoorthy, spoke of the outcomes that resulted in the "New GE Beliefs" and included values: Customers determine our success, stay lean to go fast, learn and adapt to win, empower and inspire each other, and deliver results in an uncertain world. They reflect a renewed emphasis on acceleration, agility, and customer focus. GE wanted to move its culture from Command and Control to one of Inspire and Connect—a cultural change from within (versus top-down) (Stevenson, 2014).

I was lucky enough to be at GE during this transition and I also attended two senior executive- level leadership development programs at Crotonville. From these courses and my time helping embed the new GE beliefs in my own global teams, I became intrigued on what competencies are needed to effectively lead in the twenty-first century. I developed the concept of Leaderocity™ and the notion of leading at the speed of now. I came to realize that the intersection of leadership and velocity could provide insight into the challenges facing leaders. I have spent the past few years thinking, researching, and asking what is needed.

This book is the initial result. My co-authors and I offer our set of 10 leadership competencies that we feel are pivotal for today's leaders. We are not taking the position that this is THE set or even an exhaustive inventory. We do, however, offer them as a foundation that global leaders can use to establish their leadership brand and enhance their leadership practices.

It is also especially timely in the midst of the global COVID-19 crisis and the need for effective leadership at all levels. We can see both the critical need for these competencies and the stark contrasts in practice—those leaders who are rising to the moment and others whose lacking is disappointingly notable.

I also decided that this book would be a good learning process for one of my graduate classes at Rutgers University. The notion was to "crowdsource" this book and add in the perspectives of my 15 co-authors. Our team brainstormed the book concept, topics, and the overall tone and approach. We divided the tasks among Strategy, Editorial, Creative, Research, and Content teams with 2 to 3 of us collectively authoring each chapter. The result is this compendium of 10 leadership competencies that we propose for consideration for leading in the twenty-first century.

Dr. Richard Dool

CHAPTER 1

Context

The Speed of Now

We're called on to be prepared for the challenges of a rapidly changing world. This means being ready for emerging markets, adjusting our strategies, being agile and flexible, serving clients more effectively, and thinking and acting more globally.

David Seaton, Chairman and CEO, Fluor
(Axon et al., 2015)

Increasingly, the winners in today's business environment are those companies that know how to leverage complexity and exploit it to create competitive advantage.

Morieux and Tollman (2014)

Today's business environment is considered to be more complex and dynamic than ever. Forces such as technological advances and globalization have combined to create a volatile landscape with unprecedented degrees of change. This era was captured by the U.S. Army War College back in 1987, with the term "VUCA" (volatility, uncertainty, complexity, and ambiguity), and now in 2020, seems even more so (U.S. Army Heritage and Education Center, 2018).

This period has also been called a "permanent white water world" (Vaill, 1996), "the age of turbulence" (Greenspan, 2007), and the "age of chaotics" (Kotler and Caslione, 2009).

Leaders today face a macro-environment filled with an unprecedented level of active "stressors" (e.g., technological advancement, increased globalization, nomadic and dispersed workforce, economic shifts, increased competition, increase in overall pace, increased diversity, disruptive innovations; Manciagli, 2016; Volini et al., 2019; Volpel, 2003). It is being routinely argued that the rate of change is increasing (Axtell et al., 2002).

We are in this era of "now." We are surrounded by "instant" access and response. Examples abound from text messaging, self-service checkouts, automatic bill paying, and instant quotes for services. Companies are striving hard to save seconds on transactions to create competitive advantages. Time has become a prized asset and is clearly worth more to an array of stakeholders who seem to want it "now."

In a world with a 24 × 7 orientation, reduced barriers of time and space due to technology-driven reach and access and systemic impatience, speed is more important than ever. Agility and flexibility have become critical leadership and organizational competencies. To become truly agile, an organization must embrace speed as a reality and infuse their operations with speed and dexterity with a strong dose of constant vigilance to changes in the ecosystem. Companies must be flexible to alter approaches and methods in response to new intelligence.

Organizations today are under intense scrutiny from a variety of stakeholders, including customers, suppliers, employees, regulators, community activists, and governance officials. Lombardi (1997, p. 1) dubbed this "The Spotlight Era." Systemic impatience due to the "now" orientation has led to a constant demand for results.

There is a need for leaders to be able to lead at speeds that may have been uncomfortable in the past. Patience may not be the virtue it used to be, nor can leaders be passive in this environment. Leaders must find a way to balance speed with discipline, foresight, common sense, and purpose.

HP (2004) stated: To succeed, you must balance multiple conflicting objectives—maximize return, mitigate risk, improve performance, and increase agility. All of this has to be accomplished in the midst of an unprecedented amount of change.

Two big challenges characterize leadership today. One is the need to juggle a growing series of paradoxical demands (do more with less; cut costs but innovate; think globally, act locally). The other is the unprecedented pace of "disruptive change," which speeds up the inter-action of these demands and simultaneously increases the pressure on organizations to adapt (Kaiser, 2020).

White (2006) spoke about this very well: "adaptability, tenacity, cour-age, endurance, humor, tolerance for ambiguity and the capacity to live in paradox are all needed as we move into the ever-shifting present."

Covey noted,

The first reality is change, and global competition is an embodi-ment of change. It's analogous to permanent white water, which is a turbulent, disheveling, noisy world that cannot be predicted in any way. And everyone is living in that kind of a world—in a level of change, and a rapidity of change, beyond any possible imagina-tion. (Quality Digest, n.d.)

This rapid pace of change, and the challenges of technology, globaliza-tion, and competition are changing the workplace and demand new lead-ership competencies or at least an evolution of traditional competencies. There is more expected of leaders today. They must lead and deliver results against this demanding, fast-paced, and impatient backdrop.

Win Elfrink, chief globalization officer at Cisco stated:

We are witnessing the biggest economic, social and demographic shifts in history. Aging and shrinking populations will result in fewer workers, innovators, and consumers while the emerging markets in hypergrowth areas will reinvent how business has been done and revolutionize the workforce of the future. We are now immersed in the fourth phase of globalization, what I like to call the globalization of the corporate brain, which is about co-creation and talent for companies. The new workforce will overturn many traditional attitudes about workers, working, and the workplace. But to assess what these changes entail, we need to think globally. (2020, p. 5)

Managing employees in a changing environment requires that lead-ers are competent in responding to the demands of the transitional work environment, or an environment that is subject to evolve. This suggests that many of the traditional levers of leadership may no longer be as effective. The key is to be open to change and responsive in general, lowering internal "drag" and friction points. Companies need to be "aerodynamic" (Poscente, 2008).

In his book, *Seismic Shifts* White notes:

> The future belongs to the fast. We face a clear choice, to be shaped by events that are unfolding around us, to shape them. Shaping the events will take leadership—leadership that is not authoritarian, but that leads with authentic authority. It will take leadership that helps to create and bring about a vision that will evolve as it unfolds. (2006, p. 3)

Change does not always come naturally in many organizations, it demands consistent and persistent leadership intervention.

Russell Reynolds noted:

> Uncertain times can severely test (and reveal) the quality of an organization's leadership. It is during these times that great leaders act—and act decisively. Through their actions, they set an example for everyone in the organization and stand as the difference between thriving in a crisis or suffering irreparable damage. (2016, p. 2)

Ancona captured much of what we hope to offer in this book.

> Leadership is about making things happen, contingent on a context. Leaders may create change by playing a central role in the actual change process, or by creating an environment in which others are empowered to act. Leadership develops over time. It is through practice, reflection, following role models, feedback, and theory that we learn leadership. (n.d., p. 1)

She also argues that leaders in business settings need four key leadership capabilities—sensemaking, relating, visioning, and inventing—to be successful and need to cycle through them on an ongoing basis. Added to these capabilities is the notion of a "change signature" your own unique way of making change happen. (n.d., p. 2)

In our selected competencies, we have embraced and included Ancona's capabilities.

Raia (2018) noted:

Great leadership in times of chaos and crisis is invaluable, yet it's also not an innate trait. If you're a new leader, you should feel confident that you can cultivate the necessary skills to navigate any organizational challenge. It's one thing to effectively manage people and set a positive example under optimal conditions. To do so under the most taxing kind of pressure, however, is another thing entirely. Intense strain can reveal fissures that leaders never knew existed, ultimately leading to devastating mistakes and judgment lapses.

Raia captures a key objective of our book, to offer suggested competencies for leaders to reflect upon, learn from, and potentially deploy in their leadership context. The best leaders are ever-learning, always striving to learn from others and to build up their resiliency.

Today's leaders are having to deal with degrees and shades of complexity that they have never faced before, an enormous problem if their outlook happens to be restricted or confined (Cisco, 2020).

Researchers at The Conference Board identify "ability, engagement, and aspirations" as critical managerial dimensions, with ability now including not only intellectual and technical skills, but also emotional or social intelligence. Throughout the coming decade, leadership roles will evolve to reap the benefits of the radical changes occurring in workforces and organizational structures. Leaders will concentrate much more of their energy on cultivating a culture that functions as the organization's collective consciousness and underlying value system (Cisco, 2020).

One core attribute of leadership in the future will be to bring smart people together to think in more fluid, dynamic ways, and to solve problems that have never been solved before. Leaders will need to architect creative cultures that can constantly produce new ideas and new skills.

Annmarie Neal, VP of Talent Management and Development, Cisco

Erickson (2010), who has authored several books and articles on generations in the workforce, points out that what we've thought of as leadership skills—setting direction, having the answers, controlling performance, running a tight ship—are less relevant in an environment of constant change. Increasingly, leadership is about creating a context for innovation and inclusion in the face of ambiguity and the unexpected.

It is against this backdrop that we offer our suggested competencies for leaders in the twenty-first century.

CHAPTER 2

Leader as Visionary

Richard Dool and Keisha Dabrowski

The very essence of leadership is that you have to have vision.
You can't blow an uncertain trumpet.

Theodore Hesburgh

Introduction

We define leader as visionary as a leader who is inspired and driven by the potential of the organization and works to get all stakeholders on board. They can see beyond the ambiguity and challenges of today to an empowering picture of tomorrow (Jeffrey, n.d.). This leader looks at the big picture and has the foresight to usher in change in the organization. These leaders promote unity and characteristically bring cohesiveness to inspire everyone to be on the same page. They seek information, and input from everyone, and understand that in order to achieve their vision, they need buy-in from the stakeholders involved.

Vision is at the core of leadership. The leader's job is to create the vision for the organization in a way that will engage both the imagination and the energies of its people. Vision can be the single attribute that separates good leaders from average ones and most leaders from managers.

Successful leaders of organizations that thrive in today's highly competitive and challenging marketplace are those who have created and implemented a vision and mission for the organization. An overwhelming consensus among leaders is "without vision, little can happen." All enterprises, big or small, begin with the belief that what is merely an image can one day be made real (Kouzes and Posner, 1995).

Collins (2001), who presented the traits of 11 outstanding companies in his book *Good to Great*, maintains that focused, disciplined thought is a common element of good-to-great leaders and their companies. Great leaders focus their firms on a single, organizing idea that unifies and guides all decisions.

SHRM (2018) defines vision as: "A vision statement looks forward and creates a mental image of the ideal state that the organization wishes to achieve. It is inspirational and aspirational and should challenge employees."

Many leaders have vision. What sets the best leaders apart is their ability to develop and advance that vision into action and results. A strategic, visionary leader is able to strike a balance between being a dreamer and an implementer, and know when and how much to focus on the short term versus the long term.

Hedges (2018) noted that high among leadership expectations is the ability to develop and share a vision. The visioning process is challenging; it demands a lot of a leader.

The vision should be as follows:

Future Oriented

A vision lives in the future. It's about movement—toward a goal, betterment, growth, or success. This requires a redefinition of focus for most new leaders. Coming up through the ranks as an individual contributor, we're focused and rewarded for execution, an endeavor that exists primarily in the present. Leaders need to stay aware of current objectives, but they must also be looking out toward a future that lies further ahead. Leaders have to see it first and be able to orient everyone else toward it.

Context Creating

The leader has to take the roadmap for the company and make it relevant for the team. And because we don't just exist within our companies, a good leader also provides context to the outside environment. In this way, a vision creates shared meaning for others.

Positive

We don't want to run toward a future that's dark, so a vision needs to be positive. Visionaries communicate possibility. Instead of fixating on problems, they envision solutions. This doesn't mean a vision shouldn't be based in reality. Visionary leaders see the challenges, but instead of getting down, they get focused. This type of positivity is contagious— so much so that it inspires others to be equally positive. When times get tough, their vision allows a team to cohere and push through the tribulations.

Inclusive

One dispiriting aspect of work is that you can't always tell why your work matters in the greater whole. The "cog in the wheel" syndrome undermines innovation, creativity, and job satisfaction. Working for a leader with a vision helps everyone to see how their work connects to larger objectives. Visions are intentionally inclusive. They paint a picture where everyone has a role that's meaningful and important. Again, even if this feels obvious to you, it doesn't mean that others see it. In order for a vision to truly come to life, a leader must consistently and urgently share that vision with others.

Active

Leaders have to actively keep the vision alive through action. A vision that's carefully developed and then rarely discussed is pointless. Most visions fail because leaders get bored of talking about them.

Strong visions aren't rolled out so much as woven into the fabric of the work. If leaders want the vision to stick, they need to bring it into conversations and presentations at every opportunity. In fact, they must make it a personal tagline.

Role of Organizational Vision

Atland (2015) captures the role of vision in the organizational dynamic well.

> Every organization exists for a purpose. Some organizations and
> their leaders skillfully position their reason for existence central to
> everything they do. The organization's purpose engages people. It
> drives all daily activity within and for the organization. The pur-
> pose helps to define the organization's culture.

He offers the "V-M-V-C" model to capture vision's primary framing
role and how it fits with the other elements.

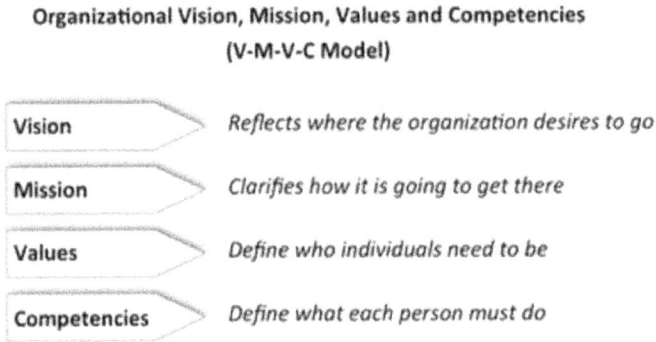

**Organizational Vision, Mission, Values and Competencies
(V-M-V-C Model)**

Vision	*Reflects where the organization desires to go*
Mission	*Clarifies how it is going to get there*
Values	*Define who individuals need to be*
Competencies	*Define what each person must do*

The first element in the V-M-V-C model is the organizational vision. The
vision clearly states the direction of an organization, their magnetic north.

The second element of the model is an organization's mission. The
mission is similar, and connected to, its vision statement. The vision
defines where the organization wants to go, and the mission clarifies how
it is going to get there. The mission statement is a roadmap for reaching
the organization's desired destination. It is a translation of the vision into
something time bound and tangible.

The next element of the V-M-V-C model is the organization's set of
values. Values shift the focus from the greater organization to the individual. Values define who individuals need to be to achieve the organization's
vision and/or live out its mission. Values articulate a set of desirable traits
or characteristics that people can exemplify in their faithful service to the
organization and its cause.

The last of the model's four elements are competencies. An organization's competency framework centers even more on the individual. Competencies define what each person must do to live the organization's values, journey along the mission, and strive to attain its vision. Competencies are action oriented. Competencies are behavioral, meaning that an individual will demonstrate them by what they say or do.

A clearly expressed vision, mission, set of values, and competencies is vital to an organization's ability to position itself in the marketplace. Strategic visions have real value when they become embedded in the "DNA" of the organization and the minds of its members who then can translate the vision into tangible actions and behaviors toward meeting specific strategic goals.

The leader is the central energy source for embedding the vision into the "DNA" of the organization from conception to execution.

Three Primary Roles of a Visionary Leader

In promoting its Strategic Leadership and Management program, Michigan State University (2020) captured the three key roles of visionary leaders.

Visionary Leaders See the World Differently

Visionary leaders can often see what no one else sees, finding potential and opportunity in a time of change or even company contraction. They see what's not there—or what's not there yet. A visionary leadership style embraces the unknown as a blank canvas for innovation, experimentation, and pioneering new possibilities. In order to cast that larger vision for a team or organization, that often means having the ability to look at the situation—whether it's an organizational restructure or diminishing product sales—in a different light, even when there seems to be no light at all.

Visionary Leaders Help Others See the Vision

For teams working in the midst of change or grasping to understand their role within the larger vision, it can be hard to see that grand vision. This is when visionary leaders have to become people uniters, bringing teams and entire organizations together and leading them in a common direction. This can play out in different scenarios with visionary leadership style tapping into the flair of storytelling or symbolism to paint a powerful picture that energizes people toward the future goal.

Visionary leaders recognize that the individual, collective team, and even an entire nation must align with the vision, have a clear goal, and understand their role in making this vision for the future a reality.

Visionary Leaders Turn the Vision into Reality

Innovative ideas and grandiose vision are meaningless if not followed up by action. The flair and charisma so often associated with the visionary leadership style must be balanced by discipline, focus, and a specific course of action.

A visionary leader ensures the vision becomes reality by stating clear goals, outlining a strategic plan for achieving those goals, and equipping and empowering each member to take action on the plan at the organizational, team, and individual levels.

Key Attributes of an Effective Leader as Visionary

There are many views on what is needed to effectively lead an organization. We would argue that being able to create a compelling vision is a core attribute. This section is our compilation of some of the key attributes based on the experiences of the leaders we interviewed and our research. It is not meant to be an exhaustive list, but more of a set of foundational (core) attributes that each leader can leverage to enhance or extend their vision competency.

Essential Traits of Effective Visionary Leaders

Through our research, leader interviews, and experience, a set of personal traits that effective visionary leaders seem to embody emerged.

Essential personal traits	
Inspirational	They ignite passion. They drive our emotions in the right direction to bring out the best in us. Effective visionary leaders have the ability to cause others to see where they are going and agree to the move toward the new vision.
Imaginative	They value innovation and imagination and allow themselves to dream, exercising their mind's eye to see beyond what's in the physical world at the moment. Visionary leaders are focused on moving past the status quo and ushering in new projects, acquisitions, or initiatives.
Persistent, resilient, and resolute	Realizing the vision will not be easy. With inner resolve, visionary leaders push through difficulties and setbacks. They remain agile enough to pivot and make course corrections, but they always persist. Setbacks aren't a sign of failure to them; they are mere stopping points on the way to realizing the vision. Leaders have to have tenacity and determination. They could likely be dealing with situations where they have to fight against old ideas, company politics, and external pressures.
Intelligent risk takers Courageous and bold	Moving toward a new goal or addressing a vision is a risk. There is no guarantee that strategies will work, but visionaries are comfortable with the uncertainty and take as many measures possible to ensure the plan is successful. As such, they are willing to take calculated risks and endure uncertainty. As a result, visionary leaders need to be comfortable with failure and volatile effects due to changes. They do not use blame as a currency, mistakes or failures are seen as a natural part of the process and sources of learning. They need to be bold and willing to go first before others, but with a dose of realism and pragmatism. They will certainly need courage of conviction as naysayers stand in the way.
Magnetic and inclusive: Skilled communicators	Visionary leaders are inclusive, inviting others to make the vision their own. They attract talented people who are passionate about what they do, who are inspired by the company's big picture. They create thriving, innovative cultures where individuals have the freedom to create their best work and take pride in their efforts. Visionary leaders bring out the best in their people.
Positivists	Visionary leaders hold a positive outlook for the future. They are hopeful they will achieve success. They don't see problems as personal, permanent, or pervasive. Instead, they are impersonal, temporary, and relate only to the present situation. These leaders are driven to create more value but are content where they are now. Their optimism is infectious throughout the organization.

(continued)

Essential personal traits	
Adaptability and agility	Leadership agility is the ability to effectively lead organizational change, build teams, and navigate challenging business conversations. The agile leader has the ability and capacity to assess risk, decide courageously, and act quickly to meet the rapidly changing environment while producing results and developing others' capacity to do the same. Agile leaders are like a camera with a really zoom lens: they have the capacity to focus on an important issue, zoom out to see the larger context, and zoom in again.
	It's in the combination of consistency and agility that leaders can become strategic, performing an organization's purpose with excellence but changing course when the situation demands.
Discipline, focus, and example	A primary task of leadership is to direct attention. To do so, leaders must learn to focus their own attention. A visionary leader's actions speak volumes and affect other people. To this end, a leader must be disciplined to ensure that the actions that are exhibited affect people positively. They must live the vision every day and be consistent in attitude, words, behaviors, and actions.

Compiled from various sources (Agility11, 2018; Coleman, 2017; Jeffrey, n.d.; Mollor, 2019; Toreto, 2017; Statusnet, n.d.)

Zwilling (2015) makes the point—"It's true that gifted visionaries bring many good things to an organization, including big picture ideas, seeing around corners, and a hunter mentality. Yet they also come with a set of shortcomings." He goes on to identify five shortcomings of a visionary: "Staying focused and following through, too many ideas and an unrealistic optimism, cause organizational whiplash, don't manage details and hold people accountable and tends to hire helpers and not develop talent."

Summary

Lavinsky (2013) noted:

> Vision in business requires that you clearly see where you choose to be in future and formulate the necessary steps to get your organization there. Creating and sustaining a vision for an organization calls for discipline and creativity.

> A business leader must have the passion, strength of will, and necessary knowledge to achieve long-term goals. A focused individual

who can inspire his team to reach organizational goals is a visionary business leader.

Visionary leaders create excitement, positive momentum, and longevity in an organization. People enjoy working for visionary leaders who truly want them to reach their full potential and find meaning in their work. Visionary leaders inspire, encourage, empower, and equip their team members.

Visionaries wear many hats with ease and live with character and conviction that results in real and positive change. The ultimate role of the visionary is to be the person who inspires change and solutions in an organization, industry, or the world.

Visionaries see things differently and must be able to communicate what they see clearly, as well as why it is important (Kinsey, 2018).

Key Takeaways

- Visionary leaders "see" into the future, often before others. Visionary leaders have outsight and can see patterns in the abstract.
- Because of the "future" aspect of vision, these leaders are willing to go first, take intelligent risks, and have the courage of conviction to offset the inevitable naysayers.
- Visionary leaders must be able to create a compelling vision, communicate it effectively to drive buy-in and then lead its execution to reach the expected outcomes.
- Visionary leaders are resilient, adaptable, and agile. They stay steadfast on the vision, but also will adjust as conditions emerge.

References

Agility11. 2018. "Leadership Agility in a Nutshell." https://www.agility11.com/blog/2018/12/28/leadership-agility-in-a-nutshell, (accessed April 5, 2020).

Atland, B. 2015. *Engaging the Head, Heart and Hands of a Volunteer*. Sarasota, FL: Peppertree Press LLC.

Coleman, J. 2017. "The Best Strategic Leaders Balance Agility and Consistency." https://hbr.org/2017/01/the-best-strategic-leaders-balance-agility-and-consistency, (accessed April 6, 2020).

Collins, J. 2001. *Good to Great*. New York, NY: HarperCollins.

Hedges, K. 2018. "Don't Have a Leadership Vision? Here's Where to Find It." https://www.forbes.com/sites/work-in-progress/2018/10/25/dont-have-a-leadership-vision-heres-where-to-find-it/#6b79ce28a0a8, (accessed April 6, 2020).

Jeffrey, S. n.d. "10 Attributes of Visionary Leadership for Change Agents and Outperforming Entrepreneurs." https://scottjeffrey.com/visionary-leadership/, (accessed March 27, 2020).

Kinsey, A. 2018. "What Is Visionary Leadership?" https://bizfluent.com/info-8721665-visionary-leadership.html, (accessed April 6, 2020).

Kouzes, J., and B. Posner. 1995. *The Leadership Challenge: How to Keep Getting Extraordinary Things Done in Organizations*. San Francisco, CA: Jossey-Bass.

Lavinsky, D. 2013. "Are You a Visionary Business Leader?" https://www.forbes.com/sites/davelavinsky/2013/04/26/are-you-a-visionary-business-leader/#512107077bbf, (accessed March 30, 2020).

Michigan State University. 2020. "What are the Qualities of a Visionary Leader?" https://www.michiganstateuniversityonline.com/resources/leadership/qualities-of-a-visionary-leader/, (accessed March 22, 2020).

Mollor, C. 2019. "Why Leadership Agility Is Critical to Company Success." https://www.predictiveindex.com/blog/the-future-of-leadership-agility/, (accessed April 6, 2020).

SHRM. 2018. "Mission & Vision Statements: What Is the Difference between Mission, Vision and Values Statements?" https://www.shrm.org/resourcesandtools/tools-and-samples/hr-qa/pages/isthereadifferencebetweenacompany%E2%80%99smission,visionandvaluestatements.aspx, (accessed April 5, 2020).

Statusnet. n.d. "What Is Visionary Leadership? 7 Traits of a Visionary Leader." https://status.net/articles/visionary-leadership/, (accessed April 6, 2020).

Toreto, T. 2017. "5 Non-negotiable Attributes of Visionary Leadership." https://www.huffpost.com/entry/5-nonnegotiable-attribute_b_11582196, (accessed April 6, 2020).

Zwilling, M. 2015. "5 Shortcomings of a Visionary and How to Compensate." https://www.forbes.com/sites/martinzwilling/2015/06/16/5-shortcomings-of-a-visionary-and-how-to-compensate/#13b814094348, (accessed April 15, 2020).

CHAPTER 3

Leader as Communicator

Tahsin Alam, Zhongyao Cai, and Wendy Silverman

Most of the successful people I've known are the ones who do more listening than talking.

Bernard Baruch

It's not enough to have an ideology; you have to be able to pass it on, to infect others with your ideas.

Gary Hamel

Introduction

The key to the success of any executive is the ability to communicate effectively. Can you imagine an effective leader who is not an effective communicator? Some research suggests that leaders devote 7 of every

10 minutes of their leadership time in some form of communication (Grossman, 2017).

Leaders today must be adept at one to one, one to many, and all forms of "e" communication. Effective communication, in real time, is now not only expected, it is critical to organizational success and the leader–follower dynamic. Leaders must be adept at both verbal and written communication as well as the "softer" skills—listening, observing, and the use of questions. Today's employees demand a collaborative or mentoring leadership style. This is highly dependent on interpersonal skills.

Leaders today often pride themselves on the ability to "multitask" especially through the use of technology. Others argue that this creates superficial relationships and interactions with employees and it is far more effective for leaders to focus on the "moment" and to create meaningful interactions with employees. Leaders must be able to connect with employees, create buy-in, and affect behaviors. The best leadership attribute to do this is being an effective communicator.

Leader as communicator may at first seem to be a simple concept with little explanation needed. However, as we embrace contemporary society and its norms of electronic communication, blended teams, and multicultural approaches, the critical role of communication begins to grow in complexity. Many of the competencies discussed in other chapters of Leaderocity™ require the foundation or partnership of an astute communicator in order to fulfill their goals. What is a visionary without the communication to create buy in? How can a producer achieve results without communicating their action plans? Can an exemplar or inclusionist encourage ethical or global thinking culture without clearly communicating those beliefs to stakeholders? The leader as communicator strives for transparency, understanding, feedback, and shared meaning.

Effective communication can happen electronically, verbally, and through nonverbal messages. Whichever medium is being used to communicate, it is important to employ caution to avoid miscommunication or misunderstanding. Body language, terminology, and attempts at using humor can easily lead to misunderstanding when engaging across generations, cultures, or language barriers (Gratis, 2018). When a leader has achieved mastery as a communicator, their messages are both clear and concise, addressing issues or goals broadly and completely.

This no-surprises attitude should come from an authentic place while demonstrating openness to feedback from their stakeholders. The communicator encourages similar behaviors in their community and ensures that alternate points of view are made welcome. While a communicator understands and acknowledges the existence of organizational hierarchies and silos, they utilize their authority to reach through these barriers to facilitate a culture of understanding and respect.

The leader should make a consistent effort to bridge the often deep gap between leadership and staff. These common hierarchical issues can impact employee engagement and retention as well as organizational culture as a whole (Maasik, 2019). Communication across different areas of the organization needs to be transparent and reliable. "Sharing data and information in a transparent manner will ensure that everyone is in the loop, and that everyone is aware of any potential issues with the business, product or service that can be addressed in a collaborative manner" (Johnson, 2020). An organization that enables cross unit communication initiatives will see more organic opportunities for collaboration as well as leadership directed connector efforts. Pettit et al. (1997) found that information transmission within an organization played an indispensable role in the process of building trust and satisfaction.

Leaders are the voice of an organization and need to be well informed in order to become better communicators. They hold influence over the opinions of internal and external stakeholders as well as potential customers. Goals for a contemporary leader include easily and smoothly communicating with others and building trust within the team, rather than just sitting in the office and giving orders. In order to use communication skills to speed up decision making, leaders should utilize a staged approach to the communication process: first, gain others' attention, second, establish awareness and understanding. Leaders can then do the third—gain the advantage of persuading others (Mai and Ankerson, 2003).

Hallmarks of Effective Communicators

These abilities galvanize communicators on their journey to expressing sincerity and confidence from the start to end of their interactions. Within that process, communicators need to listen to the audience, accurately receive both silent and spoken messages, and actively express empathy to their colleagues. Thoughtful planning before communicating, and learning to utilize nonverbal factors, along with use of supportive information can bring your progress as a communicator closer to mastery. When those unavoidable mistakes occur, trustworthy communicators should apologize as quickly as possible to reduce negative effects. This level of care brings its own set of considerations when taken digitally.

Be Honest, Don't Lie

Trust between people is very fragile. Because of implied organizational hierarchies, trust between leaders and others is often more tenuous. In today's work environment, well-utilized communication methods can promote trust between people in the organization, which can encourage collaboration and efficiency. Destroying trust can happen quickly, but maintaining it demands a long-term commitment. Communication between leaders and stakeholders, particularly those at a different level in their hierarchy will always be intimately examined for these reasons.

In addition, most people are reluctant to have in-depth conversations with people they don't believe are trustworthy. If a leader is regarded as an untrustworthy communicator, people will always be wary when talking with him whether in formal or informal settings, so he will lose many opportunities to gain helpful information from others. Narrow information channels, which are not conducive to creative thinking and decision making, will also lead to organizational failures.

Project Confidence

Vague communication tied to a lack of confidence will lead to confusion and doubts in your audience. Leaders need to demonstrate self-confidence, eagerly evaluate themselves, others, teams and organizations, and give solid suggestions. Unclear suggestions can easily lead to employees' loss of interest, or their misunderstanding, which can create drift from a specified plan of action. Therefore, when leaders articulate their requirements and goals, they need to express very clear opinions with confidence and a firm but open attitude.

When a leader issues a statement, if their attitude is lacking confidence, they may be regarded as timid or indecisive. This is not congruent with public expectations for their image and will affect not just their personal brand, but also that of the organization. Therefore, before speaking events, the leader should rehearse and gain feedback to ensure that their voice is passionate and powerful, eyes are firm, and posture is straight. This will create contagious confidence and convey a positive and upward spirit in their messaging.

Connect with the Audience

When gathering or sharing information with others, leaders need to maintain a close relationship with their audience. Outdated theories may tell leaders to keep a formal distance from employees, but distance from others will lead to abstraction, distortion, and misunderstanding in the process of information dissemination. Leaders who do not build personal relationships with others will only receive information that is repeatedly refined and purified, which creates false narratives. At the same time, leaders need to consider the human element to the audience when delivering information. We don't always have the opportunity to communicate with others individually. But no matter the size of the room or audience, effective communicators can always adjust their methods and content of information dissemination, establish close contact with everyone present, and make the audience feel a personal connection.

The Importance of Listening

Communication is multidirectional, and the role of listening is critical. When others are speaking, listening carefully demonstrates respect for one another, which is conducive to building others' interest in a further in-depth discussion. At the same time, leaders need to know when they should speak and when to stay silent. Communication is never a monologue, but works to create dialogue. A skilled communicator will make an effort to confirm that the purpose of their conversation has been achieved. In other words, they will ensure that they and their audience understand each other and a consensus has been formed. If misunderstanding exists, a good leader is not to blame the audience, but to work on their ability to receive messaging and confirm that messaging.

Empathy

Leaders need to reduce the influence of ego in the process of communication and focus on others instead. Too much self-expression and displays of one's capabilities demonstrates arrogance, which will reduce the willingness of others to communicate openly with leaders. The optimal thing to do is reduce projecting your own feelings and consider situations or messages from the standpoint of others. Empathy means putting yourself in others' shoes, which is one of the fundamental factors of communication. Empathy is also useful in solving communication problems, because expressing your understanding can calm people's anger and reduces negative emotions in the team.

Focus Your Message

When leaders communicate, they need to confirm the core intention and content of the conversations before actually talking with others, instead of casually attempting an unpracticed message. A key reason for this is to avoid wasting time, the other is that few people would like to spend their time on worthless communication. A common understanding is that good communicators need to communicate diplomatically with others, but that does not mean that there is no valuable truth in the messages. Leaders need to figure out the "what" and "how" in information dissemination, so as to avoid leaving the impression that they put greater emphasis on formation rather than the content.

Nonverbal Cues

As discussed in the section on connecting with your audience, good communicators will always pay attention to the reactions of their supporters. They are adept at recognizing changes in facial expression and body language. Impacts of communication are not only determined by the verbal content, but also by the whole body. Whether conscious or not, nonverbal factors exist all the time and influence the flow of communication. Even when verbal content conflicts with other nonverbal factors, people would be wise to abandon language and emphasize what may be perceived by the latter. Nonverbal factors are more difficult to control and often accurately express the real feelings that may be difficult to express, particularly with a workplace superior.

Facial expressions and actions are much more difficult to control than content or vocal tone. Leaders need to be comfortable making eye contact with an audience; eye contact is the most easily recognized nonverbal factor in interpersonal communication. A listener should look at the other person to show concern, but the speaker should take care to be culturally sensitive and not express aggression when returning a gaze particularly during one-on-one scenarios. When the speaker is ready for feedback, they can turn their eyes to their companion to demonstrate interest in dialogue. Facial expressions of a leader should be consistent with the content to be expressed, so that the leader's speech can be impactful. Body language can also reflect attitude, including use of conversational gestures to attract the audience's attention or stress certain content. Communication is an art and through the learning process, it is easy to feel overwhelmed. It includes not only the expression of language, but also the nonverbal factors that reflect a person's internalized feelings about the messages being exchanged.

Contextual Awareness

A skilled communicator can emphasize a certain meaning or the opposite by changing their volume, and the same content may have the opposite meaning in different tones. While a soft voice expresses candor and friendliness, when excited, words may seem shaky, when sympathizing, their tone will be low. The pace of speech will also affect the level of understanding of what we say. If a leader speaks too fast, it may cause the listener to feel confused and distracted, whereas speaking too slowly will cause the listener to lose focus.

In order to be a skilled communicator, many leaders will practice their pronunciation, vocabulary, tone, and posture repeatedly, but it is not enough to focus on themselves. At the same time, leaders need to consider these same factors related to their audience and be sensitive to the expressions shared by others. By perceiving the emotions, attitudes, and concerns of the audience, they can interpret messaging from the people or organizations they communicate with and adjust results or feedback they provide according to these needs. This does not advocate dishonest messaging but expressing the same information in different ways, so that the needs of the supporters may be met.

Using Supporting Content

In order to enlighten your audience and lay the groundwork for your message, a sophisticated communicator knows how to incorporate supporting content. These may include questions or humor that drive your narrative, stories, analogies, and relevant data. While simplifying complex narratives into data and charts can be very efficient, often these visual tools have their own internal logic, which must be clearly explained in order to help the audience glean understanding and knowledge. Proper oral interpretation of data and charts is necessary, otherwise these visual concepts cannot help the audience to comprehend or remember key points.

Utilizing a story can be an essential part of communicating, early speeches of former President Barack Obama began with his personal story, because it helps to draw the public ear with approachable and relatable information. Leaders should make use of this approach by incorporating stories in order to draw in the listener and promote their sphere of influence. When leaders show their own views and perspectives, they must make it concrete and visualized. If they can visualize it, it will be more influential.

Apologize and Admit Your Mistake

When leaders are hesitant to admit mistakes, the core of the problem is trust. If leaders are error prone, their supporters will lose confidence in them. But if they never admit mistakes, even when they are obvious, audience trust is equally damaged. The dilemma is obvious. When errors occur, leaders should admit their shortcomings frankly, because it will make them more relatable and trustworthy and can aid in uniting members of the team. An adept leader will find problems in the communication process before everyone realizes it. After recognizing the problem, they should also demonstrate courage to take the responsibility of solving the problem, rather than falling back on diplomatic words. But leaders should not be self-deprecating when admitting mistakes and shortcomings, because this will make leaders lose credibility in the team.

e-Communication Awareness

Digital communication platforms are growing and changing every day but the best practices for using them will vary little. Many of the prior hallmarks here are equally if not more vital when considering e-communication. Connecting with your audience through a focused, honest message will aid your communications whether a character limited tweet or an email to one or more stakeholders. Projecting confidence should not excuse neglecting common courtesies such as a greeting or closing line for an email.

Since you do not have voice modulations or body language to complete your messaging, words must carry the burden alone. As a result, clarity and focus are crucial components, including subject lines or attachment titles for emails. Your message recipient should know exactly the value of what they are receiving before even opening your missive.

Formality of your messaging will vary based on the level of personal rapport between you and your recipient. However, there are complications to consider, such as where a message may go later. If your friend is receiving a message from you that they may want to forward onto another party that is not the time to choose too casual a language or refer to unrelated personal information. If you are sending a message of introduction between people, adhere to the most formal wording that any party involved should use with the other. If you usually address someone by their first name because of your long-standing relationship but are introducing them to a new party, you would want to refer to them in that message by the title this new person will use (Doctor, Professor, Mr., Ms., et al.). This denotes a standard of respect and formality for your colleague and the newly introduced party.

Social media adds levels of complication to your communication brand. It may be wise to focus your social media use to one or two platforms in order to not be too broadly spread and be reduced to repeating messaging across platforms or being unable to respond in a timely manner. There is also a temptation to behave outrageously in order to gather attention or followers. If that is the leadership image that makes sense for your personal and professional goals then embrace that urge, otherwise proceed with caution. Occasional use of humor at the right time can lend you that approachable quality that aids in building connections. But if your attempt at humor falls flat that creates an opportunity to own your mistake. In the limited amount of time social media has existed many individuals have learned how to acknowledge past mistakes when a jest does not hold up over time. Consider also how photographs or videos shared may reflect your personal brand whether or not they include you personally.

When e-communication involves video or audio interactions, virtual meeting spaces for instance, it is important to demonstrate the same level of respect to your companions that you would in any in-person meeting. Put other devices away and remain focused on the attendees and the business at hand. If you must engage in activities that may be a distraction for others, let them know it is not a good time for you to have the camera on and disengage that device. Of course, you should always have your microphone muted when it is not time for you to speak. If you are the meeting host, get to know your platform and utilize settings such as having all attendees automatically on mute when they enter the space. Letting your colleagues know that intention in advance will allow them to enter the meeting confidently.

Leader as Communication in Action

Speaking Briefly and Effectively

In order to communicate effectively, leaders need to first consider what information they want to say and then how to present it. Steiner (2012), a Speech Language Pathologist, provides examples of how one may struggle with social language. These may include giving too much information, inappropriate use of phrases, sudden topic changes, or using difficult to follow stories to illustrate your message.

Before starting a focused conversation, leaders need to consider what core information they need to share in order to avoid the listener's attention being drawn to superfluous information. In the workplace we face a variety of competing information daily. Leaders must learn how to clearly express meticulous ideas in minimal time. In order to achieve this goal, three traps must be avoided: overexplaining, underpreparing, and completely missing the point.

Ensuring Understanding

Leaders must ensure their message is received and understood. Our definition of effective communication is when a leader's message is received and understood as intended. The only way to ensure understanding is through some form of feedback. This can be in the form of more dialogue, use of questions, or observing actions. Harnessing some key communication skills such as paraphrasing and summarizing can be used to confirm clarity on both sides of a conversation (Cserti, 2019). Gaps between management and employees can be lessened by giving attention to communication transparency, Gibson et al. (2020) stress the importance of frequent and clear communication in order to ensure that employees know their value they add to the organization. Feedback should be given regularly and include both kudos and critiques, but not at the same time. The historically popular sandwich method leaves employees with mixed messages and their perspective may encourage them to hear only the negative or only the positive, so it is best to only give one message at a time to ensure your point is clear (Gibson et al., 2020). Top behaviors associated with effective leadership include transparent communication and bringing out the best in others (Durham, 2015) and giving effective specific feedback and accolades brings both of these priorities together into one action item (Gibson et al., 2020).

It is important to keep any follow-up questions focused on the matter at hand and not to try to offer solutions quickly or downplay the importance of what you are being told. Allow yourself to feel the emotions being expressed by your conversation mate, empathy is a key towards understanding (Schilling, 2018). Understanding is not limited to a process where messages are sent and received it also delves into appropriate self-disclosure. When your employees make mistakes or face difficult problems, sharing about your own struggles or errors can help them to understand that you have been in their place. This can lead to an open culture where struggles are addressed and not exacerbated by anxiety (Miller, 2019).

Moving the Team Forward

Regardless of your role, everyone in the room can positively contribute to ensuring that meetings are facilitated properly. One of the main tasks of a facilitator can be compared with an orchestra conductor, cuing members and "guiding the use of their instruments toward the desired result" (Cserti, 2019). The facilitator can look for those nonverbal cues in the group, asking themselves if someone may be holding back a thought that they would like to contribute. They can look for context in the information being provided and restate the contributions of others in order to ensure clarity and shared meaning. Acknowledging the emotions that may be evoked is important, particularly when there is conflict among members or lack of cohesion in outcomes sought. Recordkeeping has become an important part of leadership, determining what ideas or solutions are moved forward and ensuring that notes accurately reflect the determinations of the group (Cserti, 2019). After a meeting takes place, it can be helpful to give clear communication in writing in order to ensure that members know what deliverables are expected from them (Kashyap, 2019).

The Value of Practice

How can we prepare to be better communicators? As the old joke says, "How do you get to Carnegie Hall?" The key of course is practice. Maddox (2015) suggests planning before you have a conversation and isolating your key points in advance. Think about it as the headline for your leading story. When it comes to active listening, incorporate nonverbal cues along with the words used, include emotional contexts and summarize or paraphrase what has been shared with you at the close of a conversation. Schilling (2018) recommends committing to that practice for a week consciously in order to make it a habit. If this seems awkward or uncomfortable you can tell colleagues and family members that you are working on your active listening skills and express an intention to confirm and summarize their messages.

In a group scenario you can explore facilitator recommended techniques such as the "ladder of inference" taking the time to observe the verbal and nonverbal cues of multiple individuals and how they are feeding off of or responding to each other (Schwarz, 2017). An important skill to practice is giving others the opportunity to communicate without interruption. Speaking before the other person finishes can degrade not only your communication opportunity but the level of esteem in which others believe you hold them. Try to ask follow-up questions that will add clarity or understanding instead of leading off in another direction (Schilling, 2018). Afterwards make an effort to thank people for their participation and contributions, particularly anyone who may not be as adept or frequent a contributor to the group (Cserti, 2019).

The Art of Questions

Gregersen (2018) offers several insights into the power of questions as a currency of effective leadership. "Questions have a curious power to unlock new insights and positive behavior change in every part of our lives." He argues that "the ability to continuously question everything is probably the most important attribute an effective leader possesses."

Great questions like these have a catalytic quality—that is, they dissolve barriers to creative thinking and channel the pursuit of solutions into new, accelerated pathways. Often, the moment they are voiced, they have the paradoxical effect of being utterly surprising yet instantly obvious.

In an interview with MIT News (2019), it was noted:

> The power and privilege of the C-suite can leave leaders insulated from internal trouble, external signals, and important insights. This "CEO bubble" creates a dangerous disconnect for leaders who must recognize when a major change in direction is required, yet often lack the information required to perceive a looming threat or opportunity.

While persistent CEOs may eventually get the information they request, it's the questions they didn't know to ask that often come back to haunt them. These unanticipated risks—or "unknown unknowns"—are business threats that can come out of nowhere.

Asking questions is essential in today's world where globalization, digitization, and disruption push leaders to the edge of uncertainty and urge them to figure out what they don't know they don't know—before it's too late. He offers four steps to propel conversations:

- Ask better questions: Obvious, but tricky nonetheless. He suggests the best results are achieved when you "compose and wait." Don't impatiently dive into finding an immediate solution. Pause to consider other variables that may redirect your focus in exciting new ways.
- Shut up and listen: You don't have all the answers—you need collaborative feedback. As a leader, it's important to create safe spaces for all employees to feel comfortable asking questions. Set the tone by acknowledging you're not the expert, graciously accepting feedback, and not immediately dismissing ideas.
- Pain + Reflection = Progress: Placing yourself in situations that allow you to be uncomfortable (pain) and quiet (reflection) are ideal for stimulating new questions and ideas. Embrace the awkwardness!
- Still blocked? Try Question Bursts: Our natural inclination is to (over)explain a question or a problem. This only guides others down your narrowed mental path, when the objective is to broaden it. Gather folks, state your goal, set a timer for five minutes, and let people loose with questions. *Just* questions.

Summary

Our multigenerational, multichannel, and multiplatform world today demands that leaders adapt communication styles that suit the modern workplace. In the past, setting a direction may have been enough in some industries, providing capital may suffice for others. Today, leaders are expected to be participatory leaders, personally active in communicating their points of view, identifying effective ways to interact in one-on-one and group settings, while simultaneously developing a robust and clear e-portfolio of communication platforms. Critical to becoming an effective communicator today are some core tenants covered in this chapter—active listening, body language, honesty, and humility. Without these, leaders run the risk of being seen as talking heads rather than active participants in what must be an exchange between leaders and followers. Empathy is currency, declarative commands are not. Yet in consuming all of this, it is important to remember that the vast majority of the population are not born communicators; practice still makes perfect when it comes to this critical leadership competency, and the time to start that practice is now.

Key Takeaways

- Collecting, providing, and transmitting information are the three keys to being an effective communicator of substantive material.
- Honesty and brevity are key characteristics of an effective leader's communication style.
- Often communicating is misrepresented as purely a one-way conversation. In fact, today's communicator needs to be able to read her audience as well as be an effective listener. In the twenty-first century, listening is equally if not more important than talking as it is a vehicle for mutual understanding, as is the ability to ask the right questions.
- Reading and projecting nonverbal cues, while elusive, can be mastered with practice. In an age where most communication is electronic, in-person communications will become a sought-after skill.

References

Cserti, R. 2019. "Essential Facilitation Skills for an Effective Facilitator." https://www.sessionlab.com/blog/facilitation-skills/, (accessed March 30, 2020).

Durham, T. 2015. "Building a Strong Corporate Reputation: Why We Need Leadership at the Speed of 'Now.'" https://apps.prsa.org/Intelligence/TheStrategist/Articles/view/11251/1117/Building_a_Strong_Corporate_Reputation_Why_We_Need#.XpzQQC2ZOfU, (accessed April 12, 2020).

Gibson, K., K. O'Leary, and J. Weintraub. 2020. "The Little Things That Make Employees Feel Appreciated." https://hbr.org/2020/01/the-little-things-that-make-employees-feel-appreciated?utm_medium=social&utm_campaign=hbr&utm_source=linkedin, (accessed March 16, 2020).

Gratis, B. 2018. "Overcoming Language Barriers to Communication." https://www.typetalk.com/blog/overcoming-language-barriers-communication/, (accessed April 11, 2020).

Gregersen, H. 2018. *Questions are the Answer*. New York, NY: Harper Business.

Grossman, D. 2017. "How Much Time Do You Spend Communicating?" https://www.yourthoughtpartner.com/blog/how-much-time-do-you-spend-communicating, (accessed July 8, 2020).

Johnson, W. 2020. "4 Benefits of Sharing Information in the Workplace." https://smallbiztrends.com/2017/01/benefits-of-sharing-information-in-the-workplace.html, (accessed March 18, 2020).

Kashyap, V. (2019). "Effective Communication in the Workplace: How and Why?" https://www.hrtechnologist.com/articles/employee-engagement/effective-communication-in-the-workplace-how-and-why/, (accessed March 30, 2020).

Maasik, A. 2019. "Reducing the Communication Gap between Employees and Management." https://www.entrepreneur.com/article/324731, (accessed February 15, 2020).

Maddox, T. 2015. "Brevity: 3 Tips for Speaking Less and Saying More." https://www.techrepublic.com/article/brevity-speak-less-and-say-more/, (accessed March 20, 2020).

Mai, R., and A. Akerson. 2003. *The Leader as Communicator*. New York, NY: Amacom.

Miller, S. 2019. "Inspirational Leaders Own Their Imperfection." https://www.chieflearningofficer.com/2019/11/25/inspirational-leaders-own-their-mistakes/, (accessed April 30, 2020).

MIT News. 2019. "Hal Gregersen says Questions are the Answer." http://news.mit.edu/2019/hal-gregersen-says-questions-are-answer-0517, (accessed May 5, 2020).

Pettit, J.D., J.R. Goris, and B.C. Vaught. 1997. "An Examination of Organizational Communication as a Moderator of the Relationship between

Job Performance and Job Satisfaction." *Journal of Business Communication* 34, no. 1, pp. 81-98. doi:10.1177/002194369703400105.

Schilling, D. 2018. "10 Steps to Effective Listening." https://www
.forbes.com/sites/womensmedia/2012/11/09/10-steps-to-effective-listening/#7d037fbd3891, (accessed March 16, 2020).

Schwarz, R. 2017. "The Ladder of Inference." http://www.pearltrees
.com/patlsac/ladder-of-inference/id17126136, (accessed September 28, 2020).

Steiner, M. 2012. "The Importance of Pragmatic Communication by Megan Steiner, M.S., CCC-SLP | Monocacy Center." http://monocacycenter.com/the-importance-of-pragmatic-communication/, (accessed April 10, 2020).

CHAPTER 4

Leader as Exemplar

Adam Gray and Wendy Silverman

Leadership takes many forms, including, and importantly, the quiet and subtle leadership of example.

Anthony S. Fauci (2018)

The first job of a leader—at work or at home—is to inspire trust. It's to bring out the best in people by entrusting them with meaningful stewardships, and to create an environment in which high-trust interaction inspires creativity and possibility.

Stephen M.R. Covey

Introduction

The leader as exemplar is a simple concept—an individual who consistently leads by example. Followers are then able to build a clear understanding of expectations and their congruency with a set of core values.

This example establishes a baseline for the organization and stakeholders of the expected values, culture, and performance. Leading the pack through the good and bad, employees come to leaders as their "north star" when lost or troubled. Normative behavior patterns are often passed down from mentor to mentee, many of today's leaders may have lessons gleaned from predecessors as much about what to do as what not to do.

An exemplar understands that the philosophy they embody becomes the basis for not just how they are seen as an individual, but also how the members of their organization view and respect each other and their stakeholders. Exhibiting authentic and ethical leadership does not mean that the leader is infallible. In fact, owning their mistakes and demonstrating their humanity to colleagues and subordinates allows a leader to open the door for those who need to share feedback or difficult news including the moral failings of colleagues or policies. The exemplar is focused on the needs and goals of team members and may demonstrate some overlap with other competencies from Leaderocity™ such as the talent scout or the communicator. The idealized exemplar looks to their team members as the leaders for the future, ensuring that they are given opportunities to grow and learn so that they can be better performers at their current roles and better prepared for new challenges tomorrow.

What are the benefits of leading by example and how is your valuable time well served through reviewing this chapter? While some informal or emerging leaders seem to operate instinctually, leading by example is a way to encourage leadership skill development into the daily routine of workspaces. Like Jimi Hendrix learning to play the guitar by watching someone else play the guitar—employees learn acceptable norms by watching these individuals lead by example. When employees fail to see the idealized direction of their work/organization, the leader needs to provide an example for their subordinates "set the direction by helping others see what lies ahead and rising to the challenges" (Bonilla, 2017). Another vital reason "leader as exemplar" is included as a competency is because it encompasses ethics in action. The tie between everyday behaviors and organizational culture is innate and occurs in an organic way (Katzenbach et al., 2016).

"Leaders can guide nations or businesses in either a positive or negative direction" (Bonilla, 2017) depending on the ethics of the leader. We need to ensure we have ethical leaders providing positive examples as opposed to those who demonstrate and encourage acceptance of moral failings by their decisions. For example, Alexander Hamilton was a successful driving force behind the founding government of the United States, but he also let pride drive many of his decisions leading ultimately to his death by duel and acting the way he would want all of his followers to act in his situation, leading as exemplar (Dool, 2019). Leaders both formal and informal, should understand the innate power of their position as an exemplar—that their conduct and speech sets the ethos of the organization. Modeled positive and negative behaviors that go unaddressed have implications toward dictating standards. This is where followers learn about acceptable behaviors through observation of leaders.

In essence, the leader is in the spotlight—all of their words, attitudes, and actions set the standards. They are under constant scrutiny, someone is always watching and judging, both internally and externally. Often the benchmarks set by leaders are unspoken—they are understood through actions, habits, and attitudes. It is particularly important for leaders to regularly self-assess in order to ensure the example they set is as intended and are influencing their followers positively. For example, a leader could knowingly or unknowingly set unofficial norms based on their behavior and attitude in a number of areas—style and level of formality, what they honor and what they criticize, how they spend their time, who they talk to and how, doors open or closed during the work day, their work ethic, and many others. In the context of the organization, how the leader deals with these sorts of things impacts his employees (Bonilla, 2017). We should remain mindful of the influence demonstrated both in and out of the workplace as inconsistent messaging can detract from our brand (Shedd, 2011).

Demonstrating a commitment to social justice initiatives such as gender equality in hiring and disaster response during times of crisis are ways that a leader or organization can underscore what they value (Weinstein, 2019). Creating an organization that encourages trust can lead to better employee retention and a more engaged and productive workforce overall (Zak, 2017). Further, leaders want to grow their organization and they need their employees to want that too. Demonstrating commitment to the organizational vision can facilitate that momentum in others around you. A leader can bring an entire team to a new, higher standard just by "committing to a greater challenge" that pushes themselves along with the team (Bonilla, 2017). Engaging in the challenge provides overall growth for employees, the organization, and the leader themselves.

Message Consistency

Leading by example successfully, "inspire[s] confidence with everyone in the organization at all times," instead of only being influential during occasional moments of genius (Chou et al., 2016). When leaders are able to consistently deliver inspiration and motivation, they gain the trust of their employees, whereas an inconsistent leader leaves their employees on edge and uncertain of their next action or direction. In order to inspire confidence in employees, leaders must routinely exercise consistency among all types of messages. Message consistency refers to a leader's verbal, nonverbal, and digital forms of communication with the organization. This also applies to the individual's social media presence and public associations in their private life (Kuligowski, 2019). To be a successful leader, "your word must be trusted. If you say you're going to do something, you have to do it. If you plan to meet somewhere, you need to be there." Since employees usually model the leadership they are given, consistency is an important trait to instill in an organization, in general, and important to an employee's career development (Roberts, 2016).

Consistency Provides Predictability

Inconsistency causes employees to feel stressed and experience uncertainty, which distracts them from the important task at hand—their job. In turn, this leads to poorer quality work from the employees. On the other hand, "employees perform best when their environments are predictable." Therefore, it's important that leaders behave in a consistent manner in the numerous situations they encounter throughout the organization as leader. If employees have a good idea about how their leader will respond to their questions/comments, it "increases engagement and satisfaction" between both the employee and the leader, therefore moving toward greater overall productivity. If, however, a leader acts emotionally and unpredictably "employees might be unwilling or even afraid to approach" the leader and thus lead to lesser productivity (Roberts, 2016).

Consistency Creates Personal Responsibility/Accountability

Employees expect their leaders to consistently deliver value, perform to their best ability, and meet the goals that are set for the organization and the leader themselves. In return, the leader expects "consistency in their employees' performance and deliverables." Mistakes or failures by leaders or employees must be acknowledged and where appropriate used as a learning tool. Exhibiting ownership and self-accountability allows the leader to function as leader as exemplar. This situation provides an ideal example of how employees should react in similar situations. By taking responsibility, the leader as exemplar is able to instill the trait of accountability in the organization thereby establishing behavioral consistency among the entire hierarchy/network. Leader as exemplar can be a catalyst of personal responsibility throughout the organization by having routine check-ins and meetings with employees to faults and successes in an honest, open manner. Being thorough and consistent with such face-to-face interactions between leaders and employees supplements consistent actions, attitudes, and words from leaders ensuring "no last-minute surprises and creates an environment of mutual accountability and respect" (Roberts, 2016).

Consistency Requires Dedication

All successful leaders are successful due to their initial commitment to whatever endeavor they have pursued, bought into, and consistently worked toward in order to get to their leadership role. Commitment creates consistency.

Consistency Delivers a Consistent Brand Image and Presence

Through successful leadership, a leader and his employees can provide a consistent brand image and "face of the organization." By providing customers a product or service consistent with your brand, a leader is able to create consistent value around the organization. Chairman of the Segal Companies, Howard Flurhr, says "your communication [to your team and to your customer] must be clear, consistent and repetitive over time." A successful leader can "focus on promoting a positive and consistent brand image" through means such as advertising, social media, campaigns, conferences, etc. "Common or rapid changes in your message [and the message delivery] and [brand] image distract [employees and customers] and prevents them from forming and strengthening an image of your company in their mind" (Shedd, 2011).

In order to provide message and delivery consistency, successful leaders must also explain to their employees/followers about inconsistencies and the "rare occasions [that] you may have to be consistently inconsistent"—meaning that certain unusual circumstances may "require that you deviate from your usual course of action." An example of one of these inconsistent circumstances facing a leader is when providing advice/direction/freedom to employees. Dr. James Brown of SEBA Solutions explains that "you may not be able to grant the same freedom/authority level to a project manager with 2 years' worth of experience that you would to a project manager with 13 years of experience." In this situation, a leader should realize that they have to act inconsistently and they should "offer extra communication to explain the inconsistencies," to the workforce generally, otherwise, questions concerning a leader's message consistency may arise and may result in the employees' loss of trust in the leader and the organization and possibly lead to a decrease in overall productivity (SEBA Solutions, 2016).

Generally, a leader must strive to fulfill the competencies necessary for leadership. A good leader who is a leader as exemplar, is introspective and reflective about all of the aspects of the leadership position. They understand that each of their actions, interactions, habits, attitudes, or words as leader as exemplar provides a message to the employees, the organization, and customers.

Exemplar in Action

To help illustrate the idea of an exemplar in action, I'll use one of our favorite leaders as the example. This leader is Lewis B. "Chesty" Puller.

Puller served almost four decades of service in the Marine Corps and ultimately became the most decorated American Marine in history. Puller is a great example of the exemplar in action because of his continued consistent efforts. After serving in combat he would return home to either work toward improving his own craft or give back to his organization by training other recruits. Puller's multiple deployments put on a prime display for his followers, allowing them to see a leader go into combat and return multiple times while also teaching others and honing his own skills—the ideal soldier that all of Chesty's followers aspired to be. Additionally, such dualism and capability exposed how Puller led others by setting the example through his own actions. Leading by example on a battlefield scenario may seem to set the bar impossibly high for today's business leaders (Dool, 2019).

Being "Visible"

One element of Puller's leadership style that applies to leading as exemplar that Landing (2010) noted was: "Be Visible," in the sense that physically being present to your followers/employees will engage and encourage them. When in absence, leaders cannot lead as exemplar, thus, "the less you're hidden away in meetings, or at your computer…the better off you'll be" as a leader (Dool, 2019). Chesty knew that his fellow Marines wanted a "confident commander would stop at nothing to get the mission accomplished," and he gave them that type of commander through leading as exemplar by "fighting alongside his Marines at the front," his courageous acts in combat, his prolonged service, and all accomplishments that he achieved as a leader. One of his most notable acts of leading as exemplar was in Nicaragua, where Puller "led the charges against the enemy rather than telling his men to charge while he held back." This wasn't just one act, rather, this was his leadership style in the Marines, literally leading as an example, showing his fellow Marines how it's done. When leaders try to be visible, they must take into account that as a leader they "must be exemplars of what is expected" as a walking, living, breathing example of what they want their employees/followers to be. Puller expected his men to "hit hard, hit fast, [and] hit often" at the front line—therefore, Puller took this as his responsibility as leader, to an exemplar of what's expected (Dool, 2019).

From a more symbolic standpoint as what it means to be a leader as exemplar, Nelson Mandela is the symbol of belief and determination as a leader that led by example. Being one of the biggest roles in fighting against South Africa's racist apartheid policies, Mandela was an exemplar through his retaliation against apartheid and his willingness to sacrifice 27 years in prison for the greater good of South Africa as a symbol of restriction to spark the fire in his people and encourage them to fight back against apartheid. Additionally, as a testament to his leadership, symbolism, and his level of intolerance toward apartheid, throughout his captivity, the South African "government had made several conditional offers of freedom, all of which Mandela had rejected"—proving his point and acting the way he would want all of his followers to act in his situation, leading as exemplar (Dool, 2019). Following his release from imprisonment, Mandela showed his followers to continue retaliating against apartheid, and lead as example through his work with the South African president at the time, F.W. de Klerk, which ultimately ended apartheid which "garnered them both the Nobel Peace Prize in 1993," through being an exemplar. Mandela kept pushing the envelope in leading his people by becoming the first black president of South Africa only a year later in 1994. During his presidency, he continued to lead by focusing on "reconciliation and forging a new sense of unity amongst the citizens of South Africa"—where he got to officially lead his entire country and people by example as the president—as a true exemplar would. Mandela was a symbol of freedom who told his story to the world as a prisoner, as a president, and as a Nobel Peace Prize winner, always leading by example (Dool, 2019)

Imperfect Leaders

Expectations of perfect people at any level in your organization are unrealistic and set an unattainable standard (Epley and Kumar, 2019). Instead focusing on building self-awareness and actively questioning your own potential biases allows for leaders at all levels to learn and grow through example (Kuligowski, 2019). Creating an image that is perfectly polished may seem like a tactical approach to building stakeholder confidence, but can surely backfire by making you inaccessible or not relatable for your employees (Gregersen, 2015; Miller, 2019). While it may seem like addressing errors weakens your authority "leadership requires leaders to possess the integrity, skills, and self-confidence to admit mistakes and not avoid dealing with them" (McKenna and Reeser, 2015). This also allows you or the organization to move forward without distractions from rumor or energy put into media "spin." Today's actions feed into a cycle of future movement, openness today leads to an environment of trust tomorrow. Openness "gives permission for people to approach you not only with feelings, but also with the information and suggestions that you need to become a more effective leader" (Tager, 2014). Admitting that you do not hold expertise on all topics and acknowledging and seeking out the prowess of others in the organization leads not only to better interactions and employee engagement but to better results and products (Walston, 2014). Williams (2017) reminds us that employees deserve these opportunities to grow and become their best work selves.

For leaders who see themselves as mentors or talent scouts, your followers can benefit from lessons learned from your past mistakes. Being able to share solid examples of similar struggles makes you approachable and your success attainable. This also creates a culture where anxiety can be lessened and removed as a barrier to productivity (Miller, 2019). Leaders who ask others for help encourage building of trust within the organization (Zak, 2017). Ethically minded organizations encourage open communication in order to break down silos and hierarchies (Kuligowski, 2019). Similarly, these ethical norms create an environment where members of the organization can feel comfortable bringing to light any identified issues. Employees who find themselves with a difficult issue to address to leadership have to fear potential repercussions and may decide that the timing or audience are not receptive, which result in delays or inabilities to move an issue forward to be rectified (Detert, 2018).

Bad Deeds in the Organization

Accountability is a norm not only for those in the C Suite; a leader who holds themselves to a high standard risks that credibility if the measure is not applied to all members of the organization and the mission or reward systems therein (Williams, 2017). Perception of organizational acceptance of a bottom line mentality or other similar moral failings needs to be avoided and if present, addressed. Otherwise this culture even if localized has a negative impact on employee performance and retention (Eissa et al., 2019; Mesdaghinia et al., 2019). Consider when planning reward or bonus structures for your organization the missteps taken by Wells Fargo when internal goals for account cross-selling at the branch level went awry. The resulting behaviors led to not only legal consequences and some bad press but also a culture issue where employees experienced psychological and physical trauma effects. Internal investigations had for many years identified issues with "sales integrity" and instead of addressing and preventing those cases used the situation as an unethical management training model (McLean, 2017).

It may be tempting to think that considering the ethical implications of company norms or rewards is a trendy topic that will pass. However, Kerr's (1975) seminal piece on these issues "On the Folly of Rewarding A, While Hoping for B" is regularly cited in research, over 800 times in the past 10 years. Kerr (1975) offers a message of warning on how these misguided approaches can impact organizational culture and behavior, public voting patterns, or medical recommendations.

Eissa et al. (2019) found that a relationship exists between employee perception of a singular focus on bottom line outcomes and employee disinterest in organizational citizenship behaviors such as team cohesion and collaboration. Employees with a strong moral identity have shown intent to leave when faced with an organization that accepts or promotes a focus on bottom line outcomes (Mesdaghinia et al., 2019). Even if messaging from the top of an organization sets clear ethical standards, localized norms or reward systems in middle management or one particular area of the company (sales perhaps) may need to be addressed. Peer behavior drives the tone and tolerance for dishonesty or even theft (Epley and Kumar, 2019).

How to Build This Competency

In order to represent yourself authentically within your leadership role you can work on building your self-awareness. Exploring your feelings, weaknesses, and motivations can help you to better relate to your colleagues and subordinates (Editor, 2014). Self-awareness can also be sought through asking questions and seeking feedback, sometimes this might lead to hearing negative things about how you communicate or make people feel. Or it could lead to a simple but effective change, like holding one-on-one meetings in a more casual seating space (Gregersen, 2015). Other experts suggest exploring meditation or psychometric self-assessments in order to become better familiar with not only your perspective but how it may differ from someone else's approach (Tjan, 2015). Being in touch with your value systems through activities such as journaling may also be a helpful tactic (Kankousky, 2017).

Summary

A leader's focus on ethical considerations may at first seem like setting an impossible standard, sure to backfire. The spotlight that never wanes also creates a unique opportunity to set norms beyond your organization that contribute to valuable movements whether environmental, or social justice oriented. Making a commitment to consistency in messaging allows for a culture of trust to grow where your supporters know that they can bring you errors to resolve instead of a culture of fear where mistakes are buried and allowed to fester. At the individual level a key step toward holding an exemplar status consists of a rigorous self-examination of potential biases. Of equal importance at the organizational level is an examination of reward systems and potential outcomes that are incongruent with the broader mission.

Key Takeaways

- Whether conscious or not, leaders set organizational norms with their everyday behaviors.
- Only a consistent message can lead to positive growth—the spotlight is always on.
- Inconsistency contributes to lack of employee trust, creativity, engagement, and retention.
- Demonstrating the ability to receive critical feedback can create opportunities to triage issues and a learning culture at all levels of the organization.

- Addressing past mistakes allows you to build an organization of trust and to move that organization forward.
- Tolerating bad behaviors such as dishonesty or reward systems that encourage unethical behavior at any level in the organization poisons the water.

References

Brown, J. 2016. "Consistency—A Critical Leadership Trait." https://www.sebasolutions.com/consistency-a-critical-leadership-trait/, (accessed April 20, 2020).

Chou, D., D. Chou, and Healthcare CIO. 2016. "Are You a Consistent Leader?" https://www.cio.com/article/3075850/are-you-a-consistent-leader.html, (accessed April 18, 2020).

Detert, J. 2018. "Cultivating Everyday Courage." *Harvard Business Review.* http://search.proquest.com/docview/2148943094/, (accessed April 15, 2020).

Dool, R. 2019. *12 Months of Leadership Insights—A Compendium of Leadership Lessons from 40 Leaders.* Seattle, WA: Kindle Direct Publishing.

Editor, B.N.D. 2014. "7 Tips for Leaders to Improve Self-Awareness." https://www.businessnewsdaily.com/6097-self-awareness-in-leadership.html, (accessed April 12, 2020).

Eissa, G., R. Wyland, S. Lester, and R. Gupta. 2019. "Winning at All Costs: An Exploration of Bottom-Line Mentality, Machiavellianism, and Organisational Citizenship Behaviour." *Human Resource Management Journal* 29, no. 3, pp. 469-89. doi:10.1111/1748-8583.12241.

Epley, N., and A. Kumar. 2019. "How to Design an Ethical Organization." https://hbr.org/2019/05/how-to-design-an-ethical-organization, (accessed April 14, 2020).

Fauci, A.S. 2018. "CAS Spring 2018 Commencement Ceremony." https://www.american.edu/events/commencement/2018/cas-spring2018.cfm, (accessed April 25, 2020).

Gregersen, H. 2015. What VW Can Learn from Gen. Stanley McChrystal About Imperfect Leaders. *Fortune.Com.*

Kankousky, M. 2017. "7 Strategies to Boost Your Leadership Skills Through Self-Awareness." https://www.insperity.com/blog/self-awareness/, (accessed April 14, 2020).

Katzenbach, J., C. Oelschlegel, and J. Thomas. 2016. "10 Principles of Organizational Culture." https://www.strategy-business.com/feature/10-Principles-of-Organizational-Culture?gko=1f9d7, (accessed April 4, 2020).

Kerr, S. 1975. "On the Folly of Rewarding A, While Hoping for B." *Academy of Management Journal* 18, no. 4, pp. 769-83. doi:10.5465/255378.

Kuligowski, K. 2019. "4 Things You Should Do to Be an Ethical Leader." https://www.businessnewsdaily.com/5537-how-to-be-ethical-leader.html, (accessed April 16, 2020).

McKenna, P.J., and E.B. Reeser. 2015. "Recovering from a Leadership Misstep." *Of Counsel* 34, no. 7, pp. 10-15.

McLean, B. 2017. "How Wells Fargo's Cutthroat Corporate Culture Allegedly Drove Bankers to Fraud." https://www.vanityfair.com/news/2017/05/wells-fargo-corporate-culture-fraud, (accessed April 30, 2020).

Mesdaghinia, S., A. Rawat, and S. Nadavulakere. 2019. "Why Moral Followers Quit: Examining the Role of Leader Bottom-Line Mentality and Unethical Pro-Leader Behavior." *Journal of Business Ethics* 159, no. 2, pp. 491-505. doi:10.1007/s10551-018-3812-7.

Miller, S.J. 2019. "Perfectly Imperfect Leadership." *Chief Learning Officer* 18, no. 9, p. 54.

Roberts, J. 2016. "Click to Read: Leading by Example: Why Consistency Matters." https://differenceconsulting.com/blog/leading-by-example-why-consistency-matters, (accessed April 20, 2020).

SEBA Solutions. 2016. "The Program Manage and Interfaces." https://www.sebasolutions.com/the-program-manager-and-interfaces/, (accessed September 15, 2020).

Shedd, D. 2011. "3 Areas Where Consistency from a Leader Is Critical." https://www.businessinsider.com/3-areas-where-consistency-from-a-leader-is-critical-2011-4, (accessed April 16, 2020).

Tager, M.J. 2014. "You Are Being Watched." *Smart Business Orange County* 8, no. 10, p. 7.

Tjan, A.K. 2015. "5 Ways to Become More Self-Aware." https://hbr. org/2015/02/5-ways-to-become-more-self-aware, (accessed April 12, 2020).

Walston, S. 2014. "Courageous Leadership Skills." *Personal Excellence* 19, no. 11, p. 28.

Weinstein, B. 2019. "Seven Bold Leaders Reveal How Ethical Leadership Is a Boon to Business." https://www.forbes.com/sites/ bruceweinstein/2019/10/14/seven-bold-leaders-reveal-how-ethical-leadership-is-a-boon-to-business/#3600c6b9454c, (accessed March 30, 2020).

Williams, C. 2017. "In Business, Accountability Starts at the Top." *Central Penn Business Journal* 33, no. 35, p. 12.

Zak, P.J. 2017. "The Neuroscience of Trust." https://hbr.org/2017/01/ the-neuroscience-of-trust?utm_campaign=hbr&utm_medium= social&utm_source=linkedin, (accessed April 4, 2020).

CHAPTER 5

Leader as Inclusionist

Keisha Dabrowski, Weijia Mao, and Peinong Tan

Diversity is being invited to the party; Inclusion is being asked to dance.

Verna Myers

Introduction

We define a leader is inclusionist as an individual who embraces diversity and promotes conscious inclusion and equity in their organizations. They advocate and create the conditions for all people to thrive in the organization as it is, while actively creating policies, infrastructures, and practices that change the conditions within the organization so that all social identities can thrive.

In an earlier chapter we shared that *vision is at the core of leadership.* However, we would also argue that if diversity and inclusion are not part of your vision, then you are not tapping into the full potential of the organization. The advantages of having a diverse workforce have been increasingly recognized as an organizational imperative that adds both tangible and intangible value. And while diversity cannot be ignored, the speed at which leaders must lead can cause even the most intentional and well-meaning leader to practice and support patterns of bias and exclusion that result in both human and economic impact to the organization. Diversity and inclusion at all levels of the organization will not happen naturally in most organizations—it requires consistent and persistent leadership intervention. Leaders must confront practices and policies to ensure bias has not seeped into the fabric of the organization. Bias (known and unknown) can create homogeneous work environments that inhibit diversity and inclusion at all levels of the organization.

Since the terms diversity and inclusion will be used throughout this chapter, it's important that we start off by defining them, as they are sometimes used interchangeably despite having different meanings.

Porterfield (2020) captures the definition for diversity as it relates to companies: Diversity refers to who's at work: who is recruited, hired, and promoted by a company. This includes gender, race, ability, religion, age, and socioeconomic status, among other identities.

Ferdman (2010) defines inclusion as follows:

In its most general sense, inclusion involves both being fully ourselves and allowing others to be fully themselves in the context of engaging in common pursuits. It means collaborating in a way in which all parties can be fully engaged and subsumed, and yet, paradoxically, at the same time believe that they have not compromised, hidden, or given up any part of themselves. Thus, for individuals, experiencing inclusion in a group or organization involves being fully part of the whole while retaining a sense of authenticity and uniqueness.

Maximizing the Benefits of Diversity through Inclusive Leadership

The diversity present in today's workplace is much greater than ever before. A simple Google search of current and forecasted demographic trends in the job market provides a plethora of information to support that many who might have previously faced employment challenges because of race, gender, religious beliefs, abilities, age, etc., are now in the workforce, and are highly sought-after applicants in the talent pool. In the United States, 67 percent of job seekers consider workplace diversity as an important factor when looking for jobs, and 50 percent of employees wish their workplace had more diversity (Porterfield, 2020).

According to the 2024 projected labor force data from the U.S. Bureau of Labor Statistics, the share of women in the labor force is projected to increase from 46.8 percent in 2014 to 47.2 percent in 2024, while the average annual rate increase projections for men is 0.4 percent for the same period. Additionally, men's share of the labor force is expected to decrease from 53.2 percent in 2014 to 52.8 percent in 2024. Hispanics, Asians, and the "all other groups" (those classified as being of multiple racial origin, American Indian, Alaska Native, Native Hawaiian, and Other Pacific Islander) are projected to increase their numbers in the labor force most rapidly. By 2024, Hispanics are projected to be nearly one-fifth of the labor force as a result of the fastest population growth of all the race and ethnicity groups. Despite a declining annual growth and a declining share of the workforce, White non-Hispanics will still make up about 60 percent of the labor force in 2024 (Toossi, 2015).

This data suggests that while certain demographic groups will grow more rapidly than others, compositional diversity in organization is and will continue to be something that must be leader-led. But diversity is rendered powerless without inclusion, which ensures that various social identities and perspectives are represented and valued at every level of the organization—especially at the levels where decisions are being made. A company's workforce may be diverse, but if employees do not feel safe, welcomed, and valued, that company isn't inclusive and will not perform to its highest potential.

Untapping this potential requires intentionality on the part of the leader. Inclusive leadership is critical to leveraging the potential of a diverse workforce. Enobong (Anna) Branch, PhD, Vice Chancellor for Diversity, Inclusion, and Community Engagement at Rutgers University-New Brunswick noted:

> Building a compositionally diverse team is the first step, but creating and nurturing an inclusive environment where all employees show up as their authentic selves is the manager's responsibility. Racial, gender, and other scripts govern our normal work lives, so it's a manager's role to interrupt this bias to ensure that all employees can fully show up.

While there are many benefits to diverse teams, taking full advantage of it is not without its challenges. It is not the presence of diversity by itself, but rather how it is addressed that leads to positive outcomes. Generally speaking, inclusion refers to the degree to which all employee teams are involved in their organizational structure. Inclusion is a function of connection, and how workers are integrated into the organization's cultural dynamics, leadership, and decision-making structure. People who work for inclusive leaders believe they are critical to how organizations operate in terms of decision making, accountability, and leadership. Inclusive leaders value individuals for their attributes and strengths, which helps the work environment be a place of sharing, dignity, and community. This leader motivates the team's humility and respect for the experiences of others by supporting and sharing authentic feedback. Achieving organizational goals is inseparable from establishing these connections with employees (Molinari et al., 2019).

Many researchers have focused on diversity and inclusion (D&I), in growing recognition of the positive impacts they can have on business performance and organizations. D&I are interrelated with each other: while diversity focuses on the demographics of groups, inclusion emphasizes appreciating diversity and integrating diversity into work life (Cottrill et al., 2014). Leaders need to engage individuals and groups equally in order to create a culture of inclusion in an organization. The leader must embrace and leverage the ideas and contributions of diverse groups to create the benefits that can follow.

In addition, an inclusive leader has a responsibility to be aware of micro aggression, and inequality, and resolve these issues with a sense of urgency (Molinari et al., 2019). Microaggressions are "brief and commonplace daily verbal, behavioral, or environmental indignities, whether intentional or unintentional, that communicate hostile, derogatory, or negative ... slights and insults" (Sue et al., 2007, p. 273).

Research from Deloitte's implies the importance of being inclusive and having diversity in an organization. The research shows an inclusive culture in an organization benefits three times to be high-performance, six times to be innovative, and eight times to achieve good business outcomes. Deloitte's research also shows that an inclusive leader could drive up to 70 percent on individual feelings of inclusion and increase the experience of fairness, respect, value, and belonging, psychological safety, and inspiration. In a team, an inclusive leader could increase 17 percent on team performance, 20 percent on decision-making quality, and 29 percent on collaboration. The insight of an inclusive leader could benefit the effectiveness of a team by empowering and respecting individuals; that many organizations, especially foreign ones, trending values multicultural and inclusive leaders now (Bourke and Dillon, 2018).

Zojceska (2020) suggests these top 10 benefits of workplace diversity as a result of inclusive practices below:

- Variety of different perspectives
- Higher innovation
- Higher employee engagement
- Better company reputation
- Better decision making
- Faster problem solving
- Increased creativity
- Increased profits
- Reduced employee turnover
- Improved hiring results

Key Attributes of an Inclusionist Leader

Research on the signature traits of inclusive leadership done by Deloitte Australia (Dillon and Bourke, 2016) notes six characteristics that provide a conceptual framework for developing inclusive behaviors and encouraging diversity as:

Committed

Highly inclusive leaders are committed to diversity and inclusion because these objectives align with their personal values and because they believe in the business case.

Cultivating a diverse, inclusive workforce takes time and energy, two of a leader's most precious commodities. Therefore, the motivation that fuels an inclusionist leader must be more than the business case. These leaders have a deep-seated sense of fairness that, for some, is rooted in personal experience. Inclusive leaders are exemplars (see chapter on leader as exemplar) and believe creating a welcoming culture begins with them, and they possess a strong sense of personal responsibility for change.

A true sign of commitment to inclusion is demonstrated when a leader devotes time, energy, and resources to nurturing inclusive workforces—by investing in people and inspiring others to share their passion and goals.

Courageous

Highly inclusive leaders speak up and challenge the status quo, and they are humble about their strengths and weaknesses.

Inclusive leaders demonstrate courage in two ways. First, they are change agents (see chapter on leader as change agent) and aren't afraid to challenge entrenched organizational attitudes and practices that yield homogeneity, even if their recommendations are politically or culturally unpopular.

Nor are they afraid to display humility by acknowledging their personal limitations and seeking contributions from others to overcome them.

Conscious of bias

Highly inclusive leaders are mindful of personal and organizational blind spots, and self-regulate to help ensure "fair play."

Inclusive leaders understand that personal and organizational biases narrow their field of vision and preclude them from making objective decisions. They exert considerable effort to identify their own biases and learn ways to prevent them from influencing talent decisions. They also seek to implement policies, processes, and structures to prevent organizational biases from stifling D&I. Without such measures, inclusive leaders understand that their natural inclination could lead them toward self-cloning, and that operating in today's business environment requires a different approach.

Curious

Highly inclusive leaders have an open mindset, a desire to understand how others view and experience the world, and a tolerance for ambiguity.

Open-mindedness, a passion for learning, and a desire for exposure to different ideas have fast become leadership traits crucial to success, especially in challenging times. Curiosity and openness are hallmarks of inclusive leaders, who hunger for other perspectives to minimize their blind spots and improve their decision making.

In addition to accessing a more diverse array of viewpoints, inclusive leaders' ability to engage in respectful questioning, actively listen to others, and synthesize a range of ideas makes the people around them feel valued, respected, and represented. Inclusive leaders also refrain from making fast judgments, knowing snap decisions can stifle the flow of ideas on their teams and are frequently tinged with bias.

Culturally intelligent (competent)

Highly inclusive leaders are confident and effective in cross-cultural interactions

Knowledge of other cultures is essential for today's leader. Beyond "book" knowledge, cultural intelligence connotes leaders' ability to change their styles in response to different cultural norms. For example, culturally intelligent leaders who are typically extroverted and demonstrative will make an effort to show restraint when doing business with individuals whose cultures value modesty or humility. They regulate the speed and tone of their speech and modify their nonverbal behaviors—gestures, facial expressions, body language, and physical interactions—as situations dictate. In addition to understanding other cultures, these leaders also demonstrate self-awareness of their own culture, recognizing how it shapes their worldview and how cultural stereotypes can influence their expectations of others.

Collaborative

Highly inclusive leaders empower individuals as well as create and leverage the thinking of diverse groups.

Inclusive leaders understand that, for collaboration to be successful, team members must first be willing to share their perspectives. To that end, they create an environment in which all individuals feel empowered to express their opinions freely with the group. They also realize that diversity of thinking is critical to effective collaboration; thus, they pay close attention to team composition and team processes. For example, they prevent teams from breaking into subgroups, which can weaken relationships and create conflict. They also engender a sense of "one team" by creating a group identity and shared goals, and by working to ensure team members understand and value each other's knowledge and capabilities.

Besides the six characteristics (6C's) provided by Deloitte Australia, other competencies that we would offer that are critical for the inclusionist leader include:

Culturally Curious

Rosen and Digh (2001) noted: "*In the new borderless economy, culture doesn't matter less; it matters more.*" In all global organizations, leaders not only symbolize various cultures, but they lead a multicultural environment. Webb (2014) notes cultural differences are influential and leaders should be self-aware to learn other cultures to better immerse themselves. In order to recognize the cultural context and consider the uniqueness, leaders need to get familiar with various cultural models of leadership to raise their awareness and let them become sensitive. For example, the organization may guide them to develop a deeper awareness of Eastern leadership styles and the implication of Eastern culture trends. Learning from other cultures to build competency and understanding is another rational learning approach that helps leaders develop a sense of globalization.

Edgar Schein noted, "*Knowledge of other cultures begins with becoming conscious of making explicit one's own cultural assumptions. Cultural understanding and cultural learning start with self-insight.*" It is important to recognize how the culture of the organization will impact the leadership, and consider the profits that the organization gains (Webb, 2014).

An Exemplar

According to the Oxford Dictionary, exemplar means a person or thing that is a good or typical example of something. In the leadership field, there is a theory called *Trait Theories of Leadership* (Callahan et al., 2007). Trait approaches to leadership represent the first attempt to understand why some people became leaders and others did not. It shows that leaders have certain characteristics or traits that make them leaders. Traits repeatedly cited as being associated with leadership include intelligence, social skills, determination, and confidence (Northouse, 2004). Although *Trait Theories of Leadership* has been criticized by some scholars, the recognition of the basic importance of traits in understanding effective leadership has re-emerged, and traits play an important role in the development of full-range leadership theories (Northouse, 2004).

Research shows that people are spontaneously inspired by positive role models (Lockwood et al., 2002). Qualitative researchers proposed that effective leaders are exemplars or role models who use their concepts, relationships, and dramatic skills to influence others. More specifically, they can create a vision of the future, distinguish themselves from others, and reinforce people's thinking around specific values.

Managers also compare themselves to specific model leaders to assess their specific leadership skills and behaviors (Guillén et al., 2015). Managers are role models that others at work look up to. Reflecting on what kind of role models they want to be and how they want to be described by subordinates or colleagues may foster a sense of responsibility in shaping the next generation of leaders.

When your team members view you as someone they want to emulate, they're more dedicated to the company and to each other. If you expect your employees to work hard and commit themselves to your company while you fail to show the same dedication, expect turnover rates to skyrocket and work quality to plummet (Dool, 2019).

Values Difference

An inclusionist leader's role is to provide a welcoming environment that acknowledges and respects differences and helps the team to see the value in them. This idea conforms to the definition of "diversity management," which focuses on managing the differences within a company's workforce, obtaining the benefits of diversity, and diminishing workplace challenges. Appreciating differences in diversity is essential, it asks leadership to acquire and follow the competencies that will channel an individual's perspectives and understanding to create a diversity dividend (Military Leadership Diversity Commission, 2019).

In terms of cultural differences, researchers illustrate that organizations must meaningfully discuss where the differences are and how leaders leverage them for better effectiveness (Webb, 2014). Beyond an individual's gender, race, religion, or sexual orientation, other cultural differences such as thinking and learning styles, personal agendas, experiences, and conflict management style, etc.

Differences produce a process of finding objective information and decision. The University of Maine (2004) noted teams that embrace differences are usually more effective than teams created without knowledge of differences. It benefits a team or an organization since everyone is contributing and interacting effectively.

Rosinski (2009) offers the following methods for dealing with cultural differences:

1. Recognize and accept differences—acknowledge, appreciate, and understand that acceptance does not mean agreement or surrender
2. Adapt to differences—move outside one's comfort zone, empathize (temporary shift in perspective) and understand that adaptation does not mean adoption or assimilation
3. Integrate differences—hold different frames of reference in mind, analyze and evaluate situations from various cultural perspectives, and remain grounded in reality; it is essential to avoid becoming dazzled by too many possibilities
4. Leverage differences—make the most of differences, strive for synergy, proactively look for gems in different cultures, and achieve unity through diversity.

How a Leader Can Enhance or Develop This Competency

Culture can significantly affect the organization's performance, efficiency, employee morale, productivity, and the organization's ability to attract, motivate, and retain talented people (Warrick, 2017).

Leaders influence culture through their strategies, practices, values, leadership style, and example (Steers and Shim, 2013). A high level of vulnerability and humility is required to self-check and calibrate in order to lead by example. The leader needs to first realize that as they move their organization from diversity to inclusion, they are embarking on a journey that is important to the organization, but not everyone will agree. Resistance to diversity efforts in organizations is a well-established and a ubiquitous phenomenon (Kidder et al., 2004).

There are two theories or concepts, the critical race theory and intersectionality, that may be of interest to leaders as they consider their approach to D&I.

Critical race theory (CRT), which originated in the 1980s, is a remaking of critical legal research on race and the possibility of changing the relationship between law and racial power, and more broadly pursuing programs of racial liberation and anti-subordination. CRT is a collection of critical stances against the existing legal order from a race-based point of view (Brooks, 1994). It examines the emergence of race and racism in mainstream cultural expressions. In adopting this approach, CRT scholars have sought to understand how victims of systemic racism are influenced by racial and cultural perceptions and how they can represent themselves against prejudice.

Almost at the same time as CRT, the concept of intersectionality is widely concerned by scholars. The term intersectionality was specifically coined and developed by the critical race scholar Kimberley Crenshaw (1989, 1996) to solve theoretical legal problems and to work within and against the law. Crenshaw uses the metaphor of the crossroads to describe and explain the intersection of racism and sexism.

Ange-Marie Hancock (2007) recently pointed out that intersectionality is not only a normative theoretical argument, but also a research paradigm. On this basis, as an analytical framework widely applicable to all kinds of marginal and privileged relationships, intersectionality can be incorporated into mainstream social science research and knowledge construction.

Phoenix and Pattynama (2006) pointed out intersectionality foreshadows a richer ontology, rather than an attempt to lump people into one category at a time, which treats social status as a relationship, and it makes visible the multiple orientations that make up daily life and the power relations at its core.

Additionally, an inclusive philosophy is emerging and thriving. It is making progress because it conforms to a philosophy of liberal political systems and multiculturalism: a philosophy that celebrates diversity and promotes fraternity and equality of opportunity. Inclusion must be at the core of any society that values these values (Thomas, 1997).

Inclusionary Leader in Action

As noted in the introduction, this book is being written during COVID-19, a once in a century global pandemic, that has disrupted work as we know it and has altered regular life and organizational cultures in ways that have yet to be determined or understood.

Government regulations implemented to minimize the spread of the virus by social distancing has closed schools, businesses deemed nonessential, and moved work online.

The diversity within organizations and the practice of inclusion is vital in this moment as leaders are challenged to look at problems differently and consider impacts that we might not otherwise have to acknowledge.

With thousands of lives being lost, and deep human suffering currently occurring, the psychological costs associated with being a member of a historically marginalized group in the workforce is high (Seng et al., 2012). The negative health consequences of social inequality have been well established in the United States (Wilkinson, 2005).

In a *Harvard Business Review* article titled, "How to Be an Inclusive Leader Through a Crisis," workplace culture and human capital strategist, Daisy Auger-Dominguez states, "Now is a time for leaders to think about what type of leader they need to be for all of their workers, especially the most vulnerable and marginalized" (Tulshyan, 2020).

Through both observed and personal experience here are examples of ways that leaders are engaging in inclusive practices during this time:

Ensuring that all employees have equal access to home internet, computers, and other resources needed to work from home.

Making virtual meetings equitable by providing different means of training on use of technology, turning on closed captioning, sending documents, and collecting input in advance.

Checking in with employees who may be disproportionately impacted by this crisis for a number of reasons including, home-schooling parents, targeted minority groups, and those with chronic health conditions, and older staff members who may be more susceptible to the virus.

Understanding how bias may show up, and managing how they are perpetuated within the team.

Inviting those on the team that may have typically not been included to meetings as part of the team brainstorming. Beginning meetings with acknowledging everyone in the room, not just those with high status or privilege.

Showing understanding and compassion. Some employees may be dealing with a number of personal issues that include mental health, competing needs, etc. during this time.

Finally, providing opportunities for employee voice to gain insightful feedback, and course correct to ensure that they are getting the professional support needed to perform in this critical time.

Resources and Other Tools to Support the Journey

Being an inclusionist leader is about the journey not the destination. This leadership skill must be developed on a continuum, as the leader must constantly be listening, learning, and adapting to be more inclusive. Claiming to have nice thoughts on diversity, creating a committee or hiring someone to do the "diversity and inclusion work" will not suffice to being an inclusive leader without personal commitment.

D&I is courageous work. It requires humility on the part of the leader to acknowledge their own biases and be open to receiving feedback on their blind spots. As Brené Brown shares in her book for developing brave leaders and courageous cultures, choosing your own comfort by opting out of vital conversations about diversity and inclusivity because you fear looking wrong, saying something wrong, or being wrong is the epitome of privilege. Doing this will break down trust especially within a diverse organization, and move you away from meaningful and lasting change (Brown, 2018).

While we will offer some tools here to support your journey, it's important to note that to be an inclusionist leader requires consistent and ongoing personal development in order to then support the development of the organization.

Bourke and Espedido (2020) offer three tactics to support inclusive leadership development:

> Establish a diverse personal advisory board (PAD)—a diverse group of people, who have regular contact with the leader and whom the leader trusts to talk straight. These trusted advisers can give leaders granular feedback on everyday interpersonal behaviors that support or inhibit inclusion.

> Openly share your learning journey about recognizing and addressing biases. This helps leaders to test and build on their insights and role model the importance of humility in addressing biases.

> Immerse yourself in uncomfortable or new situations which expose you to diverse stakeholders. Exposure, combined with open-ended questions, helps to expand horizons and disrupt preconceived ideas.

Summary

Diversity is increasingly becoming something that leaders cannot avoid in order to navigate today's complex organizational challenges. While there are both tangible and intangible benefits of organizational diversity, the benefits demand persistent and intentional leader interventions. A leader's attitude toward difference is a significant variable, the inclusionist leader sees diversity and inclusion as an organizational asset to be championed and leveraged to create sustainable organizational competitive advantages.

Leaders must be culturally open, curious, knowledgeable, respectful, aware, and ultimately savvy in this new century being an inclusionist leader is a journey, not a destination. This leadership skill must be developed on a continuum, as the leader must constantly be listening, learning, and adapting to be more inclusive. Claiming to have nice thoughts on diversity, creating a committee or hiring someone to do the "diversity and inclusion work" will not suffice to being an inclusive leader without personal commitment.

Key Takeaways

- Benefiting from diversity will not happen naturally, it is a leader-led process.
- An inclusionist leader embraces diversity and promotes conscious inclusion and equity on their teams.
- Being an inclusionist leader is necessary to keep up with the ever-evolving demographics of the workforce.
- Six traits of inclusive leaders are: commitment, courage, conscious of bias, curious, culturally open, courageous, and collaborative.
- Being an inclusionist leader is about the journey not the destination, so commitment is key.

References

Bourke, J., and A. Espedido. 2020. "The Key to Inclusive Leadership." https://hbr.org/2020/03/the-key-to-inclusive-leadership, (accessed April 20, 2020).

Bourke, J., and B. Dillon. 2018. "The Diversity and Inclusion Revolution: Eight Powerful Truths." https://www2.deloitte.com/us/en/insights/deloitte-review/issue-22/diversity-and-inclusion-at-work-eight-powerful-truths.html, (accessed April 20, 2020).

Brooks, R.L. 1994. "Critical Race Theory: A Proposed Structure and Application to Federal Pleading." *Harvard BlackLetter Law Journal* 11, p. 85.

Brown, B. 2018. *Dare to Lead: Brave Work, Tough Conversations, Whole Hearts*. New York, NY: Random House.

Callahan, J.L., J.K. Whitener, and J.A. Sandlin. 2007. "The Art of Creating Leaders: Popular Culture Artifacts as Pathways for Development." *Advances in Developing Human Resources* 9, no. 2, pp. 146-65.

Cottrill, K., P.D. Lopez, and C.C. Hoffman. 2014. "How Authentic Leadership and Inclusion Benefit Organizations." *Equality, Diversity and Inclusion: An International Journal* 33, no. 3, pp. 275-92.

Crenshaw, K., N. Gotanda, G. Peller, and K. Thomas. 1996. *Critical Race Theory. The Key Writings that Formed the Movement*. New York, NY: Free Press.

Dillon, B., and J. Bourke. 2016. "6 Characteristics of Inclusive Leaders." https://deloitte.wsj.com/cio/2016/05/04/6-characteristics-of-inclusive-leaders/, (accessed April 20, 2020).

Ferdman, B.M. 2010. "Teaching Inclusion by Example and Experience: Creating an Inclusive Learning Environment." In *Leading Across Differences: Cases and Perspectives—Facilitator's Guide*, eds. B.B. McFeeters, K.M. Hannum, and L. Booysen, pp. 37-50. San Francisco, CA: Pfeiffer.

Guillén, L., M. Mayo, and K. Korotov. 2015. "Is Leadership a Part of Me? A Leader Identity Approach to Understanding the Motivation to Lead." *The Leadership Quarterly* 26, no. 5, pp. 802-20.

Kidder, D.L., M.J. Lankau, D. Chrobot-Mason, K.A. Mollica, and R.A. Friedman. 2004. "Backlash toward Diversity Initiatives: Examining the Impact of Diversity Program Justification, Personal and Group Outcomes." *International Journal of Conflict Management* 15, no. 1, pp. 77-102. doi:10.1108/eb022908.

Lockwood, P., Jordan, C., & Z. Kunda. 2002. "Motivation by Positive or Negative Role Models: Regulatory Focus Determines Who Will Best Inspire Us." *Journal of Personality and Social Psychology* 83, no. 4, pp. 854-64.

McLaurin, J.R. 2008. "Leader-Effectiveness across Cultural Boundaries: An Organizational Culture Perspective." *Journal of Organizational Culture, Communications and Conflict* 12, no. 1, p. 49.

Military Leadership Diversity Commission. 2019. *Examples of Diversity Definitions.* Arlington, VA: Military Leadership Diversity Commission.

Molinari, C., Lundahl. S., & L. Shanderson. 2019. *The Culturally Competent and Inclusive Leader.* In Rubino, L., Esparza, S., & Y. Chassiakos, New Leadership for Today's Health Care Professionals, 2nd Ed. (pp. 49–67). MA: Jones and Barlett.

Northouse, P. 2004. *Leadership Theory and Practice.* Thousand Oaks, CA: Sage.

OpenStax. 2018. "Diversity and Inclusion in the Workforce." https://opentextbc.ca/businessethicsopenstax/chapter/diversity-and-inclusion-in-the-workforce/, (accessed April 12, 2020).

Porterfield, S. 2020. "10 Diversity & Inclusion Statistics That Will Change How You Do Business." https://blog.bonus.ly/diversity-in-clusion-statistics, (accessed April 14, 2020).

Rosen, R., and P. Digh. 2001. "Developing Globally Literate Leaders." *American Society For Training and Development* 55, no. 5, pp. 70-83.

Rosinski, P. 2009. "Coaching across Cultures." Advanced Executive Coaching Seminar, Rosinski & Company.

Seng, J.S., W.D. Lopez, M. Sperlich, L. Hamama, and C.D. Reed Meldrum. 2012. "Marginalized Identities, Discrimination Burden, and Mental Health: Empirical Exploration of an Interpersonal-Level Approach to Modeling Intersectionality." https://www.ncbi.nlm.nih.gov/pmc/articles/PMC3962770/, (accessed April 12, 2020).

Steers, R., and W. Shim. 2013. "Strong Leaders, Strong Cultures: Global Management Lessons from Toyota and Hyundai." *Organizational Dynamics* 42, no. 3, 217-27.

Sue, D.W., C.M. Capodilupo, G.C. Torino, J.M. Bucceri, A.M. Holder, K.L. Nadal, and M. Esquilin. 2007. "Racial Microaggressions in Everyday Life: Implications for Clinical Practice." *American Psychologist* 62, no. 4, 271-86.

The University of Maine. 2004. *Appreciating Differences, Getting Things Done in Groups.* https://extension.umaine.edu/publications/6104e/ (accessed June, 20, 2020)

Thomas, G. 1997. "Inclusive Schools for an Inclusive Society." *British Journal of Special Education* 24, no. 3, pp. 103-7.

Toossi, M. December 1, 2015. "Labor Force Projections to 2024: The Labor Force is Growing, But Slowly: Monthly Labor Review." https://www.bls.gov/opub/mlr/2015/article/labor-force-projections-to-2024.htm, (accessed April 17, 2020).

Tulshyan, R. 2020. "How to Be an Inclusive Leader Through a Crisis." https://hbr.org/2020/04/how-to-be-an-inclusive-leader-through-a-crisis?utm_medium=social&utm_campaign=hbr&utm_source=linkedin, (accessed March 28, 2020).

Warrick, D.D. 2017. "What Leaders Need to Know About Organizational Culture." *Business Horizons* 60, no. 3, pp. 395-404.

Webb, L., J. Darling, and N. Alvey. 2014. *Multicultural Leadership Development in the 21st Century*. White Paper. Rockville, MD: EnCompass.

Zojceska, A. 2020. "Top 10 Benefits of Diversity in the Workplace." https://www.talentlyft.com/en/blog/article/244/top-10-benefits-of-diversity-in-the-workplace-infographic-included, (accessed April 3, 2020).

CHAPTER 6

Leader as Ambassador

Stephanie Dresher and Saumil Joshi

Awareness is fine, but advocacy will take your business to the next level.

Joe Tripodi

Introduction

Leaders today have an evergrowing responsibility to represent and embody the company, brand, or organization they represent. This kind of ambassadorship may have existed in one form or the other in the past, but in the information intensive twenty-first century and the related scrutiny, it has become a nonnegotiable leadership demand. Such a leader is able to create, practice, and preach the vision of the organization with their actions. When one looks at the leader they are able to think of the brand they represent.

Leaders of associations, organizations, and companies must realize that the way they present themselves will tie back to the organization they represent. They are often the "face" of the organization. The leader must make sure to represent the right image and perception for the brand in all that they do and communicate. Leaders must live the values of the organization in a public and private manner consistently. In these times, advocacy and ambassadorship has changed immensely because of the rise of social media and the pace of life in the workplace today (Pributsky, 2018).

Leaders in the twenty-first century will face a lot of hurdles when trying to represent the organization and brand. There is risk in damaging the brand with one ill-timed or poorly worded tweet or Instagram post. The scrutiny leader's face has really changed the way that leaders have to be aware of what they do on a daily basis. Leaders must be able to embody and be the face of their brand despite the complexities of this chaotic environment (Pributsky, 2018). Being an effective ambassador and advocate has become a critical leadership competency for twenty-first century leaders.

The Need for Proactive Ambassadorship

In leading an organization, there are some long-standing core fundamentals expected of a leader—as examples; being morally ethical and having a deep sense and practice of integrity. To be an ambassador, there must be a direct alignment between a leader's values and that of the brand they are trying to embody and direct. The actions of a leader do not represent them alone but "they are also representatives of their team, their company culture, and their entire organization" (Conant, 2017).

The environment that surrounds leaders today puts them under a direct, continuous spotlight. Leaders today will be seen as inspirational figures if they can create a good perception of the values of their organization. Critics, competitors, and the media are constantly scrutinizing leaders or organizations and their actions (Jaramillo, 2017). Many will not hesitate to attack, criticize, or troll. For example, companies like Chick-Fil-A have faced criticism based on the CEO's social values, which resulted in a boycott of the business by some groups. The CEO, Dan Cathy, has made comments opposing gay marriage causing many to criticize Chick-Fil-A as a business at large and affecting revenue (Lucas, 2019).

Leaders like Bill Gates have largely mastered the role of ambassador for his brand. He has been named a "leadership legend" by outlets like *Entrepreneur Magazine* (Rampton, 2016) for his work in philanthropy. Gates was able to "take charge to help others by guiding them in the right direction, imparting knowledge and experience, or even providing the necessary resources that will improve the lives or careers of others" (Rampton, 2016). He has worked tirelessly to promote the Bill and Melinda Gates Foundation and the causes they support. The Gates Foundation donates billions of dollars to helping children and adults all around the world to help better their lives (Boseley, 2017).

These two examples of leaders as brand representatives show the impact of and the need for effective ambassadorship. Being a leader for an organization today demands that a leader properly consider the pros and cons of their actions and statements as it can leave an indelible mark on the organization well beyond the individual.

Key Advocacy Attributes

When considering advocacy and ambassadorship, there are some key attributes needed to be an effective leader as an ambassador. Through research and experience a leader can build these traits to effectively be an ambassador for their organization.

Attributes of an ambassador	
Passionate	Leaders who identify their passion for their work and organization and can effectively translate it to behaviors, public statements, and actions will be able to succeed in today's 24/7 news cycle. While a sense of caring can be manufactured, few things are as effective as genuine passion translated to public communications.
Knowledgeable	An ambassador is only as effective as the depth of knowledge they have at hand. Having as many answers to anticipated questions positions a leader for success and helps to avoid missteps. Preparation is key, so a leader needs to be up to speed on current discussions while also having the strength to always tell the truth.

(continued)

Attributes of an ambassador	
Professional	Being the face of a company requires the leader to constantly maintain a professional outlook on actions and words. Social media posts should be limited and relate to things that involve noncontroversial topics or topics that stand by what the brand believes.
Engaged	Having the ability to reach out to the community and gauge their views and values is important. In order to push messaging and gain traction for the brand, it is important to engage with the multiple audiences on a regular basis. Caring about your followers' opinions and needs is necessary.
Authentic	In a study done in 2016 with 2,000 consumers within the ages of 20–39, "56 percent of people admitted to cutting back or quitting social media altogether just to avoid exposure to the high volume of paid advertisements"(Stackpoole, 2017). Nobody wants to have information sent to them constantly without a true need for it. Authenticity for a leader can mean that they are able to show their pride for their company without while being authentic and to the point.
Confidence	Brand ambassadors are as effective as the confidence with which they deliver their message. Each decision should be level-headed and have a reason behind it that is evident to the community. Appropriate confidence in message delivery will in turn garner confidence by the community in the leader and company.
Commitment	Ongoing commitment in brand leadership is key, particularly given our round the clock news media and a continuous demand for updates and new information. A leader must be consistent in their representation of their business and values. Consistency comes with commitment and once a leader begins communicating to multiple audiences, they need to be committed to an ongoing communications plan.

Competency in Action

The leaders of twentieth-century century companies tended to act like a closed book while remaining off the radar of media and public presence. Even though these leaders managed major parts of the company, they were not easily accessible by the public (DeWitt, 2020). The leaders of the past did not want their personal lives exposed and did little to be in the spotlight. In the twenty-first century, things have changed. Leaders are inviting the public to have a closer look into what they believe in to help the public better connect them to their organization. Today the senior leader is expected to be visible, out-front, and the "face" of the organization (Shariatmadari, 2018).

The following are examples of how a leader's role as ambassador directly creates positive outcomes for a business:

Customers trust the human touch

In recent times, companies have started to portray their CEOs in their commercials, television advertisements, or social media posts. When customers have the ability to see the leader behind the product, they feel more inclined to become engaged with the vision statement that is communicated through these advertisements (Turner, 2018).

Represent existing customers

Today, people love to listen to the stories and personal insights of leaders. These stories can relate to their existing customers and can also be used to reach new ones (Champniss et. al., 2015). Existing customers feel valued when they can relate to a leader or can create a dialog in some form with the leader.

Extending the responsibility

While having the leader of an organization be a visible ambassador is a given, many companies have achieved gains by spreading the brand responsibility across the leadership team. For example, the CEO and founder of Facebook, Mark Zuckerberg, who has a moderate ambassador presence, has extended the responsibilities of ambassadorship to Facebook COO Sheryl Sandberg who is now the second-in-command of the company and addresses the major issues that Facebook is faced with in the public domain (Petersen, 2019). Having more voices within the organization helps a leader tell the organizational story in a more profound manner and helps reach wider audiences. The senior leader should be the main image but behind them, there should be a network that keeps the brand vibrant and well represented.

Modern Methods of Advocacy

Today's world demands the use of multiple channels of communication in order to build brand visibility and loyalty. The "leader as communicator" chapter in this book summarizes nicely the importance of the individual leader and their communication style. So far in this chapter, we have covered the leader's individual role in ambassadorship. There are, in addition, a few additional ambassadorship programs developed by today's businesses that require examination, both for their efficacy and as an extension of a leader's overall brand effort.

Brand Ambassadorship Programs

Lululemon was able to create its own brand ambassador program to further reach Lululemon customers in specific locations. These ambassadors are handpicked from local areas surrounding a Lululemon store so "they are able to tap into the community in an effective manner and are seen as a trusted source of information by that community" (Duel, 2018). Having these brand ambassadors helped Lululemon brand further spread their messaging into smaller areas. These brand ambassadors may be other staff or even external stakeholders such as customers or influencers, thereby complimenting the company leader's own ambassadorship efforts. A leader must be ready to expand their efforts and include staff and programs such as these to communicate the company's values and products. Brand ambassadors should feel a strong connection with the beliefs, values, and product of the organization (Brandchamp.io, 2020a).

College Brand Ambassadorship

A recent phenomenon in brand ambassadorship is the growth of college campus based ambassador programs (Brandchamp.io, 2020b). College campuses have a huge network of young adults where a brand can really harvest and further grow its roots. Victoria's Secret, for example, created a college brand program. The Victoria's Secret website states that you "must be able to be an on campus social media influencer, impact product design and branding, empower other young women on your campus and get real world career building experience" (Victoria's Secret, n.d.). These brand ambassadors must follow specific requirements when accepting the job. For Victoria's Secret some specifics include: frequently posting to social media for the PINK Campus Rep social channels in order to raise brand awareness, share daily style tips, throw events on campus, and most importantly sharing what is cool and trending on the college campus to the brand itself so that they can stay on trend at all times (Victoria's Secret, n.d.).

Case Study: Adobe's Social Shift Programs

As discussed above, each employee reflects the company in some way. The head of Adobe's social business center of excellence, Cory Edwards, found a way to get employees to use their social accounts in ways to build the brand. Due to one of the employee's social media efforts, the company had driven more revenues comparatively than its overall social media efforts through official profiles (Julig, 2019). Edwards realized that the flag of brand ambassadorship did not have to be in the hands of the senior leader and leadership alone. Every employee of the company has the capability to be the face of the organization. Edwards launched Adobe's social shift program to provide employees training on social media guidelines framed by the company. It shares the best practice for social media postings, sharing tips, writing blogs, color schemes, and social media policies (Borges, 2017). The following is a synopsis of Adobe's program from Borges (2017). This is a good example of embedded ambassadorship in an organization driven by senior leaders.

Adobe Brand Ambassadors

Write a Story

The Adobe social media team created a blog named "Adobe Life." Employees are encouraged to write a blog sharing the behind-the-scene view of what it is like to work at Adobe. The blog shares the perspective of an individual employee through interviews, celebration pictures, and live tweets.

#AdobeLife

Beyond their primary jobs, employees at Adobe are engaged with the brand and are involved in the overall company culture. Contests are held online and offline that challenge the workers and promotes Adobe authentically at the same time. For example, a T-shirt-designing contest was held where employees are asked to design a T-shirt that reflects the organization's culture. The winner is announced online using their social media platforms. This drives engagement by allowing the public to see in on the inner workings of the brand, as well as promoting the company's values and culture. To acknowledge the efforts of employees, the social media posts by employees using #AdobeLife are printed and put up on the bulletins at offices located worldwide. This gives a sense of ambassadorship within the office.

Use LinkedIn and Glassdoor

Employees at Adobe are encouraged to use LinkedIn proactively to share the projects they are working on, to publish posts about new things they have learned professionally and day-to-day life pictures. On the Glassdoor website, which is the most popular feedback website for corporates, employees at Adobe are asked to share their reviews about the work culture of the company.

Brand Ambassador Program

A special program launched by the corporate reputation team in September 2014 brought 21 employees together from 7 different locations that were actively participating in social media activities. These employees were given hands-on deep training to represent the company at different conferences and events.

How a Leader Develops this Competency

Leaders today need to be the face of the organization in everything they do. Today's customers are equally concerned with corporate social responsibility as well as the services that a business can provide for them. When customers are looking where to consume products they may dig deeper into the organization and what they stand for and live adopting their espoused values. Established brands like Coca-Cola, General Motors, and Adidas have a strong brand value and are of "old and trusted" roots (Michalewicz and Michalewicz, 2007). It took years for these companies to build credibility, but for emerging companies, it is not viable to wait for years to build that trust among customers because of the aggressive competitive times. In fast-moving times, a leader must convey the brand value of an organization in order to give it a competitive edge. Can you imagine companies of recent times like Amazon without Jeff Bezos, Tesla without Elon Musk, and Google without Sundar Pichai?

To infuse the trust into the credibility of the product among customers, leaders need to come out of their comfort zone and be active ambassadors. To help differentiate the organization, the senior leader needs to be more visible and active as the "face" of the organization. The following are three ways a leader can develop this competency:

Understanding Brand Ambassadorship

You may be the leader of a successful brand or a company; your sales might be strong and revenue might be up. But today's customers want to know more about the organization than just sales numbers. The senior leader is the best person to articulate the brand value of the company. In today's media-driven world, a leader needs to actively represent the organization's values and message. Think about Steve Jobs from Apple, Mark Zuckerburg from Facebook, and Bill Gates from Microsoft. People are more likely to trust these companies because they know the leaders behind the brand (Steimle, n.d.). Ambassadorship acts as a bridge between your customers and your company.

A Consistent Messaging Plan

As discussed, misplaced tweets, Instagram posts, and public appearances can result in catastrophic harm to a company and its reputation. Today's leaders should expend resources to develop a consistent, ongoing brand ambassadorship program with the assistance of communications experts. Spending money on this effort may have in the past seemed to be a less than optimal use of resources, but today, those who do spend the resources to do so reap significant benefits (Weber Shandwick, 2012). This kind of investment will maintain consistency, represent a holistic image of the brand and the leader while also infusing spontaneity in a measured fashion.

Market Yourself

Other than internal meetings and events of the company, a leader will represent their company at various events and conferences they attend. A leader carries the organization's values by presenting it when attending various events and networking conferences. Within today's society, each moment is captured and put up on social media outlets and press outlets to further help the leader gain exposure for their brand (Barney, 2019)

Summary

The leader must perform tasks that strategically represent the brand and company at all times. Stakeholders and customers put their trust into a company that has a strong-minded senior leader with similar values as the organization itself. The senior leader is not the only person that should exercise ambassadorship, but the employees should try their best to also represent the organization. Each employee has the ability to show his or her brand ambassadorship through his or her online presence in today's society. An ambassador truly carries the company's value wherever they go, leaving footprints behind. In order to be an advocate for a company, the leader must embody the same values that the company values within their everyday life. The leader should act as the company's face through their individual actions.

Key Takeaways

- The actions of a leader do not only represent them but also represent the whole organization.
- A leader as an ambassador's top priorities is to show passion, knowledge, and professionalism.

- Brand ambassadorship programs are key within large labels today to be able to be more in tune with smaller and niche communities.
- A leader needs to be the primary brand ambassador of an organization, but the employees who have embraced the values of an organization can represent the brand in their individual networks.

References

Barney, J. April 3, 2019. "Omnipresence in Marketing: The Power of Being Everywhere (and How to Get There)." https://www.einstein-marketer.com/omnipresence-in-marketing/, (accessed May 9, 2020).

Borges, B. April 3, 2017. "Integrating Social Media Across the Enterprise at Adobe [Podcast]." https://www.socialmediatoday.com/news/integrating-social-media-across-the-enterprise-at-adobe-podcast/502320/, (accessed March 24, 2020).

Boseley, S. November 28, 2017. "How Bill and Melinda Gates Helped Save 122m Lives – and What They Want to Solve Next." https://www.theguardian.com/world/2017/feb/14/bill-gates-philanthropy-warren-buffett-vaccines-infant-mortality, (accessed May 13, 2020).

Brandchamp.io. April 17, 2020a. "Guide to the Lululemon Ambassador Program." https://brandchamp.io/blog/lululemon-ambassador-program/, (accessed May 18, 2020).

Brandchimp.io. April 1, 2020b. "The 5 Best College Brand Ambassador Programs." https://brandchamp.io/blog/college-brand-ambassador-programs/, (accessed March 11, 2020).

Champniss, G., H.N. Wilson, and E.K. MacDonald. (October 12, 2015). "Why Your Customers' Social Identities Matter." https://hbr.org/2015/01/why-your-customers-social-identities-matter, (accessed April 22, 2020).

Conant, D. 2017. "The Best Leaders Are Ambassadors." https://conantleadership.com/the-best-leaders-are-ambassadors/, (assessed September 24, 2020).

DeWitt, P.M. 2020. *Instructional Leadership*. Thousand Oaks, CA: SAGE Publications.

Duel. November 22, 2018. "5 Successful Brand Ambassador Program Examples (including, Lululemon, Red Bull, Harley Davidson)." https://

www.duel.tech/blog/5-successful-ambassador-programs, (accessed April 24, 2020).

Jaramillo, K. December 12, 2017. "5 Reasons Business Leaders Should Share Press Coverage on Social Media." https://powderkeg.com/5-reasons-business-leaders-share-press-coverage-social-media/, (accessed April 24, 2020).

Julig, L. January 10, 2019. "4 Ways to Turn Your Employees into Brand Ambassadors: Social Media Examiner." https://www.socialmediaexaminer.com/turn-employees-brand-ambassadors/, (accessed April 22, 2020).

Lucas, A. November 20, 2019. "Chick-fil-A No Longer Donates to Controversial Christian Charities After LGBTQ Protests." https://www.cnbc.com/2019/11/18/chick-fil-a-drops-donations-to-christian-charities-after-lgbt-protests.html, (accessed May 1, 2020).

Michalewicz, M., and Z. Michalewicz. 2007. *Winning Credibility: A Guide for Building a Business from Rags to Riches*. 2nd ed. New York, NY: Credibility Corporation Pty Ltd.

Pributsky, D. December 6, 2018. "Your Startup Needs Brand Ambassadors Now More than Ever—Here's How to Get Them." https://www.entrepreneur.com/article/324374, (accessed March 23, 2020).

Rampton, J. September 9, 2016. "How Bill Gates Became a Leadership Legend." https://www.entrepreneur.com/article/250607, (accessed May 12, 2020).

Shariatmadari, D. February 22, 2018. "Privacy is Starting to Seem Like a Very 20th-century Anomaly | David Shariatmadari." https://www.theguardian.com/commentisfree/2015/nov/07/privacy-seems-20th-century-aberration-but-worth-mourning, (accessed April 18, 2020).

Stackpoole, J. August 1, 2017. "The 5 Most Important Traits in a Brand Ambassador."https://www.eventprostrategies.com/the-5-most-important-traits-in-a-brand-ambassador/, (accessed May 11, 2020).

Steimle, J. n.d. "Should Your CEO be the Face of Your Company?" https://www.joshsteimle.com/influence/should-ceo-be-face-your-company.html, (accessed March 24, 2020).

Turner, D. July 5, 2018. "Emerging Company CEOs as Chief Brand Ambassadors." https://medium.com/@Dave_BlackCow/emerging-company-ceos-as-chief-brand-ambassadors-2cbcea942b07, (accessed May 1, 2020).

Victoria's Secret. n.d. "PINK Nation: Campus Reps." https://pink. victoriassecret.com/pink-campus-reps, (accessed May 13, 2020).

Weber Shandwick. 2012. "The Social CEO: Executives Tell All." https:// www.webershandwick.com/uploads/news/files/Social-CEO-Study. pdf, (accessed May 11, 2020).

CHAPTER 7

Leader as Change Agent

Richard Dool and Stephanie Dresher

Progress is impossible without change; and those who cannot change their minds cannot change anything.

George Bernard Shaw

Introduction

We define the leader as a change agent, as the catalyst for change. A leader is one who inspires and convinces constituents that change is necessary, gets others to buy-in, reassures, follows the change through to completion, leading the execution to meet the expected outcomes.

If one accepts that continuous change is at least, in part, a macro-environmentally induced condition, and will be for some time, this state of constant change, the associated stressors, and the persistent change initiatives launched in response, may increase employee stress and have a deleterious impact on employee productivity and job satisfaction.

Additionally, well-intentioned, but poorly positioned and executed change management prescriptive programs, implemented in response to changes in the environment, may also contribute to an increase in employee stress. This may lead to a condition hypothesized as "enervative change" (Dool, 2007).

Leaders in the twenty-first century must perform effectively in a variety of roles to meet the unique demands created by this macro-environment. Given the systemic impatience in many of the organization's stakeholders, the pace of the environment, and the advances in technology, it could be argued that the ability to lead change effectively is one of the key roles of leaders. Effectively leading change translates into a range of best practices from creating the change vision, communicating the change, leading a "guiding coalition" (Kotter, 1996), mitigating risk, and controlling the by-products of change (e.g., employee stress). Leaders must be able to embed resiliency into the organizational culture and to reposition change as a natural organizational process. Being an effective change agent as a leader has become a critical leadership competency for twenty-first century leaders.

Change Realities

What Are the Drivers of Change

It has been argued that leaders today face an environment filled with an unprecedented level of active "stressors" (e.g., technological advancement, increased globalization, nomadic workforce, economic shifts, increased competition, increase in overall pace, increased diversity, social media, war for talent, and systemic impatience) (Tucker, 2019; World Economic Forum, n.d.; Anthony, 2018; Lambertson, 2018). It is being routinely argued that the rate of change is increasing (Alton, 2018; Mann, 2017; Elle, 2017). Many of the challenges organizational leaders face today are the same as in past decades but the pace and complexity of changes are of a magnitude never before experienced (Bruce, 2018; Pendleton, n.d.). It appears that many of the stressors occur simultaneously or at least have significant overlap.

The presence of the macro-environmental stressors suggests that most organizations will have to adjust (change) to meet these conditions in such a manner that will either be continuous or so frequent as to seem continuous (Mingardon et al., 2018). The demands of the organization's stakeholders and market forces create pressure on management to act.

Palmer and Dunford (2002) identified a set of environmental pressures for change as well as organizational pressures. The environmental pressures include fashion pressures (imitating competitors), mandated pressures (legal or regulatory), geopolitical pressures (realignments), hyper-competition pressures, and reputation or credibility pressures (crises). The organizational pressures include growth, integration, identity, new CEO, and power or political pressures. Ouye (2011) identified five trends as drivers: the continuing distribution of organizations, the availability of enabling technologies and social collaboration tools, the coming shortage of knowledge workers, the demand for more work flexibility, and pressure for more sustainable organizations and workstyles.

What Does Change Really Look Like

Organizations are undergoing a distinctive and rapid pace of change (Paredes, 2019; Burns, 2009) with an estimated 46 percent of organizations undergoing three or more complex change programs at one time (indicating a need for leaders to accept change as normality (Baumgartner, 2019).

Palmer et al. (2009) posit the main types of changes tend to be driven by three common organizational, or structural changes that include downsizing or rightsizing, technology or systems changes or realignments (mergers, acquisitions, or divestitures). A fourth could be added with leadership changes (CEO). Palmer et al. (2009) further argue that organizations generally face what they labeled as "first-order" (incremental change) or "second-order" (discontinuous change) (p. 86).

First-order changes can be either anticipatory or reactive. They are generally small-scale changes and often a result of individual initiatives or from the development of local practices or routines. These are often changes resulting from tuning, improving, enhancing, or developing. They are adjustments that are intended to support organizational continuity and order. Second-order change is transformational or radical. These types of changes alter the organization and include discontinuous practices such as delayering, outsourcing, disaggregation, down scoping, and changes in internal boundaries (Palmer et al., 2009).

Palmer et al. (2009) go on to note these second-order changes can be characterized as "tectonic" change (large enough to overcome inertia), "punctuated equilibrium" (short bursts of fundamental change), and "robust transformation" (enactment of new capabilities).

Walkme (2020) identified five types of organizational changes: organization-wide, transformational, personnel, unplanned, and remedial. Organization-wide change is a large-scale transformation that affects the whole company. Transformational change specifically targets a company's organizational strategy. Personnel change happens when a company experiences hyper-growth or layoffs. Unplanned change is typically defined as necessary action following unexpected events. Leaders implement remedial changes when they identify a need to address deficiencies or poor company performance.

Much of the literature related to organizational change focuses on large-scale changes and neglects the micro-changes that also create stress for employees. Sikora et al. (2004) note that employees today face numerous daily stressors related to change as well as major upheavals (e.g., mergers).

Too often leaders become impatient with results, while under pressure from stakeholders and launch serial change initiatives. This can lead to a condition of *Change Fatigue*$^{TM.}$ (Dool, 2007).

Why Do So Many Change Initiatives "Fail"?

Research indicates that change initiatives fail at a high rate (70 percent) (Asher, 2018; Gleeson, 2017; Anand and Barsoux, 2017). Change initiative failures occur for various reasons including poor strategy decisions or lack of vision, inappropriate choices, poor monitoring and control, lack of resources, leadership impatience or underestimation, neglected stakeholders, the lack of a unifying framework for action, a shift in conditions, the lack of holistic integration, poor execution or poor design, and communications (Dickson, 2019). Blanchard (2010) found that 29 percent of change initiatives are launched without any formal structure whatsoever. Failed change initiatives may contribute to employee stress by undermining the employee's capacity to absorb and respond to more change.

Another potential cause of change failures is the variable of resistance. In addition, Hatman (2009) as cited in Rosenberg and Mosca (2010, p. 140) note that individual or personal factors for resisting change came in two dimensions: active and passive. Resistance to change is often cited by leaders as the reason for change failures (Erwin and Garmon, 2009). Leaders believe workers resist change and as a result do all sorts of things to counter that resistance. But instead of breaking through resistance, leaders may *create* it. People resist being controlled.

Because people do not resist change, they resist *being* changed. Resistance to change is hard to assess, measure, and monitor. Rigid change leadership and management initiatives, with chain-of-command type governance, are often undermined by key stakeholders who resist planned change with skilled use of power, influence, and resources.

In summary, leaders must understand their impact on change success. Leadership mistakes or impatience often leads to change failure. In their rush to change their organizations leaders end up immersing themselves in an alphabet soup of initiatives. Serial changes due to leadership impatience undermine the ability of the organization to sustain change.

Effective Change Agents

The Dual Role of the Leader as Change Agent

Effective leaders of change must serve equally as agents of change and protectors of continuity.

Samuel Wilson

The art of progress is to preserve order amid change, and to preserve change amid order.

Alfred North Whitehead

During times of change, leaders have a dual role. Change does not come naturally to many organizations or individuals. As we learned from Lewin (1947) and Schein and Schein (2016), organizational culture is a powerful force for inertia in an organization. Leaders have to perform two distinct roles in times of change. They must be a source of discomfort or urgency to shock the system to break down inertia and the natural tendency of the organizational culture to fight change. At the same time, they must also be a source of psychological comfort "that we can do this." They need to be a source of "pragmatic positivism." They need to be confident, consistent, and positive that the change initiative will work while also layering in doses of pragmatism, realism, and adaptability.

The Three Key Actions of Leaders as Change Agents

The new leader is one who commits people to action, who converts followers into leaders, and who may convert leaders into agents of change.

Warren G. Bennis

In times of change, leaders have three distinct, but connected responsibilities. They must:

- Create a compelling change vision
- Communicate the change vision in such a manner as to create broad and deep buy-in across and down the organization
- Lead the execution of the change vision to reach the expected outcomes and to embed the associated changes into the organizational DNA.

Essential Traits of Effective Change Agents

There are many views on what is needed to effectively lead change. This section is our compilation of some of the key attributes based on the experiences of the leaders we interviewed and our research. It is not meant to be an exhaustive list, but more of a set of foundational (core) attributes that each leader can leverage to enhance or extend their change agency competency.

Research and experience offers a set of personal traits that effective change leaders seem to embody.

Essential personal traits	
Courageous	Change can be hard and leaders need to have courage of conviction to see it through. They need a backbone and a willingness to go first and navigate the naysayers who inevitably surface. Embarking on change means choosing at times uncertainty and discomfort. As a change agent, you're also creating those conditions for others, which might not be popular. It takes courage to break out of the norm and to speak out to people who may not want to hear the truth.
Optimistic	Change creates stress and natural inertia will seek to fight it. Leaders need to be present change in a positive light, "we can do this" but also be grounded with doses of realism and pragmatism.
Patient	Change usually takes longer than expected and one of the main reasons for change "failures" is leadership impatience. Leaders need to be patient to see the change through and to fully embed it. They need to avoid the "serial change" syndrome by shifting too quickly.
Resilient	Virtually no change initiative will go as planned, there is always some drift as conditions change or some highs and lows as the change is manifested. Leaders need to stay the course and not overreact to the inevitable highs and lows. Effective change agents don't take the lows or resistance personally. Instead, they bounce back and don't quit when they hear "no." Resilience enables the persistence required to drive change.
Deliberate	Change leaders need to be strategic, intentional, and deliberate. Change is a leader-led process. To influence change, you must deliberately choose the words and actions that break the patterns so change can happen. Change leaders need to take on a persona of being calm, confident, and in control.
Empathetic	Change agents must be able to put themselves in other people's shoes to understand their experience. You must predict how people will feel about change even if you don't feel that way. Empathy stops you from judging people for resisting change, so you can recognize that their response to change is normal and valid. Effective change agents help employees understand what's in it for them and use that to drive buy-in.
Grit	Angela Duckworth argues that an individual's grit is a better predictor of long-term success, more than talent or IQ. Grit is a combination of passion and perseverance for long-term goals. She notes "I do mean hard work and not quitting things when they're hard, but I also mean passion." Change leaders need to have some grit to overcome the obstacles that likely will emerge. Agarwal (2019) defined it as a growth mindset, the resilience that makes a leader determined to bounce back from failures and setbacks.
Flexible	We call this "focused flexibility," meaning that leaders need to stick to the change vision and plan, but also be flexible enough to adapt as conditions warrant. They have to be committed to their change vision, but too much in love with it. They have to actively monitor the change initiative and be willing to shift when it warrants—shifting both too early or too late can have unintended consequences.

Leading Change—People and Process

The Center for Creative Leadership (n.d.) offered these practices as a frame for leading process change:

> Strategic change doesn't happen on its own. Effective leaders guide the process from start to finish. Here are the three key competencies that are part of leading the process:
>
> - Initiate. Effective change leaders begin by making the case for the change they seek. This can include evaluating the business context, understanding the purpose of the change, developing a clear vision and desired outcome, and identifying a common goal. Unsuccessful leaders say they didn't focus on these tasks enough to reach a common understanding of the goal.
> - Strategize. Successful leaders developed a strategy and a clear action plan, including priorities, timelines, tasks, structures, behaviors, and resources. They identified what would change, but also what would stay the same. Leaders who weren't successful said they failed to listen enough to questions and concerns, and failed to define success from the beginning.
> - Execute. Translating strategy into execution is one of the most important things leaders can do. In our study, successful change leaders focused on getting key people into key positions (or removing them, in some cases). They also broke big projects down into small wins to get early victories and build momentum. And they developed metrics and monitoring systems to measure progress. Unsuccessful change leaders sometimes began micromanaging, got mired in implementation details, and failed to consider the bigger picture.

They also offer these three skills for leading the people side of change. Researchers found that three skills provide the necessary connection between the process part of change and the people part of change. These three C's unite effective change leadership:

1. Communicate. Unsuccessful leaders tended to focus on the "what" behind the change. Successful leaders communicated the "what" *and*

the "why." Leaders who explained the purpose of the change and connected it to the organization's values or explained the benefits created stronger buy-in and urgency for the change.

2. Collaborate. Bringing people together to plan and execute change is critical. Successful leaders worked across boundaries, encouraged employees to break out of their silos, and refused to tolerate unhealthy competition. They also included employees in decision making early on, strengthening their commitment to change. Unsuccessful change leaders failed to engage employees early and often in the change process.

3. Commit. Successful leaders made sure their own beliefs and behaviors supported change, too. Change is difficult, but leaders who negotiated it successfully were resilient and persistent, and willing to step outside their comfort zone. They also devoted more of their own time to the change effort and focused on the big picture. Unsuccessful leaders failed to adapt to challenges, expressed negativity, and were impatient with a lack of results.

Adding to the CCL suggestions, we offer these practices deployed by effective change leaders.

Leading change—Best practices	
Communicate, communicate, communicate	Some leaders in times of change revert to a "need to know" or "information is power" style of communication. Just the opposite is needed. Leaders need to overcommunicate, using every available medium or tool in a creative yet repetitive and overlapping manner.
	Engage, engage, engage. Leaders often make the mistake of imagining that if they convey a strong message of change at the start of an initiative, people will understand what to do. Nothing could be further from the truth. Powerful and sustained change requires constant communication, not only throughout the rollout but after the major elements of the plan are in place. They also need to create active and engaged bidirectional communication channels that encourage input, dialog, and feedback.

(continued)

Leading change—Best practices	
Relentless champion and evangelist	Change is a leader-led process, it can't be done from afar. Leaders need to be the "face" of the change and out-front. They need to be relentless change champions and evangelizing the "why" of the change and the expected outcomes at every opportunity.
	Become a change storyteller. To keep people committed for the long haul, they need to know what's happening and what's meaningful about that. They also need to be able to help create and tell the story. Don't make the mistake of assuming progress updates need to all come from the executive level.
	Make the rational and emotional case together. Leaders will often make the case for major change on the sole basis of strategic business objectives. Such objectives are fine as far as they go, but they rarely reach people emotionally in a way that ensures genuine commitment to the cause. Human beings respond to calls to action that engage their hearts as well as their minds, making them feel as if they're part of something consequential.
Consistent and persistent—living the change	Change does not happen naturally in many organizations. For change to fully embed and the expected benefits gained, leaders need to be consistent and persistent. They need to be shining exemplars of the change, living it daily. They need to be consistent in attitude, words, behaviors, and actions. Any inconsistency will sow confusion and inertia. Critical to the success of any change initiative is ensuring that people's daily behaviors reflect the imperative of change. Effective change agents start by defining the critical few behaviors that will be essential to the success of the initiative. Senior leaders must visibly model these new behaviors themselves, right from the start, because employees will believe real change is occurring only when they see it happening at the top of the company.
Culture Fit	Lou Gerstner, who as chief executive of IBM led one of the most successful business transformations in history, said the most important lesson he learned from the experience was that "culture is everything."
	Skilled change managers, conscious of organizational change management best practices, always make the most of their company's existing culture. Instead of trying to change the culture itself, they draw emotional energy from it. They tap into the way people already think, behave, work, and feel to provide a boost to the change initiative. To use this emotional energy, leaders must look for the elements of the culture that are aligned to the change, bring them to the foreground, and attract the attention of the people who will be affected by the change.

Leading change—Best practices	
Early and meaningful participation	Kotter (1996) noted the need for a "Guiding Coalition." Effective change agents recruit key, influential employees across and down the organization and involve them early in the change initiative. They give them opportunities for meaningful participation in order to drive buy-in, ownership, and ensure a highly likelihood for successful implementation. Change has the best chance of cascading through an organization when everyone with authority and influence is involved. In addition to those who hold formal positions of power—the company's recognized leaders—this group includes people whose power is more informal and is related to their expertise, to the breadth of their network, or to personal qualities that engender trust. Change leaders often fail to take into account the extent to which midlevel and frontline people can make or break a change initiative. The path of rolling out change is immeasurably smoother if these people are tapped early for input on issues that will affect their jobs.
Assess and adapt	Many organizations involved in change efforts fail to effectively measure their success before moving on. Leaders are so eager to claim victory that they don't take the time to find out what's working and what's not, and to adjust their next steps accordingly. This failure to follow through results in inconsistency and deprives the organization of the needed information about how to support the process of change throughout its life cycle.
	Effective change agents create a set of appropriate and relevant metrics (aka KPIs, Milestones, CSFs) and track them systematically. They use them for a variety of purposes—to track progress, to serve as an early warning system, to create momentum, to offer proof for naysayers and to celebrate small wins on the path to the full change. If something drifts, they assess and potentially adapt as needed.
Drive collaboration	Paul Pellman, CEO of Kazoo shared, "The management of it shouldn't be siloed in leadership. The biggest mistake I often see in change management is that company leaders often fail to involve managers in the process to embrace, promote, and facilitate the changes that need to happen." It is critical to bring managers into the process early and often. When managers aren't completely aligned or involved with the organizational change, employees hear mixed messages and feel ambivalent toward the initiative. This also applies to appropriate other internal and external stakeholders.
	Change agents who resist early engagement at multiple levels of the hierarchy often do so because they believe that the process will be more efficient if fewer people are involved in planning. But although it may take longer in the beginning, ensuring broad involvement saves untold headaches later on. Not only does more information surface, but people are more invested when they've had a hand in developing a plan. One common aphorism in change management is "you have to go slow to go fast."

(continued)

Leading change—Best practices	
Embed change into the a organizational DNA	It will usually take longer than many leaders seem to understand to fully embed the change initiative into the organizational DNA. Change agents have to ensure the changes are fully embedded into the practices, processes, and systems of the firm. Leverage formal solutions. Persuading people to change their behavior won't suffice for transformation unless formal elements—such as structure, reward systems, ways of operating, training, and development—are redesigned to support them. Many companies fall short in this area.
	Leverage informal solutions. Even when the formal elements needed for change are present, the established culture can undermine them if people revert to long-held but unconscious ways of behaving. This is why formal and informal solutions must work together.
	By asking people at every level to be responsible for quality—and by celebrating and rewarding improvements—change leaders are able to create an ethic of ownership in the change.

The Adaptive Leader

Shifting Change from a Noun to a Verb

As noted earlier, many firms are launching persistent (serial or overlapping) change initiatives in response to stressors in the environment. Clearly, one way to reduce the negative effects of *continuous change* is to reduce the number of change initiatives launched by the organization. If recent history is a guide, this seems unlikely. The systemic impatience between organizational leaders and their stakeholders as well as the volatility in the environment indicates that depending on a reduction in change initiatives is not a reasonable position. It would certainly help and should be encouraged but another approach needs to be pursued.

An alternative to reducing the number of change initiatives is to reframe the notion of "change" and to create a change leadership framework that encourages a more adaptive and flexible organization.

One of the challenges to the interpretation of the theoretical change models is that it is often assumed a "one-size-fits-all" approach. This is unrealistic. Change may have many common characteristics, but in practice, change is a situational and a specific experience for employees and the organization.

The research into the "adaptive enterprise" may offer a template for a new change management. A key to becoming an adaptive enterprise is to reframe the notion of change. Instead of treating change as an unusual organizational response, change is reframed as a natural part of the organization's fabric. Change is repositioned as an organizational asset allowing the firm to seamlessly adapt to changing conditions. Sikora et al. (2004) argue that change should be repositioned as an active verb instead of a noun.

The adaptive enterprise is one that not only successfully weathers change in the environment, but one that leads the charge through the change and comes out on top (Lyteson, 2016).

In this environment, one must adapt and survive, as firms must react to changes in the marketplace in real or near real time. The threats in the environment have reached unprecedented proportions. Examples that have emerged include hyper-competition, cyber criminals, malicious insiders, technology failures, social media trolling, and data theft (Smith, 2018; Irwin, 2017).

The adaptive enterprise would be better suited to reduce the negative impact of the frequent daily stressors. The point of the reframing of change is to create an environment where change becomes part of the organizational DNA and often takes place unintentionally as employees go about doing their jobs. This view of change also reshapes the impact of stress because change becomes more "natural."

An "adaptive" approach to change that improves the organization's flexibility, and agility as well as reducing the stress related to change, may offer a solution to the negative aspects of *Change Fatigue*^{TM} (Dool, 2007).

Leaders today need to have to have a high "adaptability quotient" (AQ). Adaptability quotient, is a subjective set of qualities loosely defined as the ability to pivot and flourish in an environment of fast and frequent change (Murray, 2019). "IQ is the minimum you need to get a job, but AQ is how you will be successful over time," Fratto notes:

> AQ is not just the capacity to absorb new information, but the ability to work out what is relevant, to unlearn obsolete knowledge,

overcome challenges, and to make a conscious effort to change. AQ involves flexibility, curiosity, courage, resilience and problem-solving skills too. (Murray, 2019)

Amy Edmondson, a professor of leadership and management at Harvard Business School, says it is the breakneck speed of workplace change that will make AQ more valuable than IQ. Learning to learn is mission critical. The ability to learn, change, grow, experiment will become far more important than subject expertise (Murray, 2019).

Of course, the adaptive leaders and enterprise are not immune from a macro-change event (e.g., merger or economic shock). These would have to be addressed directly. The adaptive organization's frame of reference is geared toward ecosystem integration and its execution focus moves past reacting to change or managing change to seamlessly adapting to change.

A New Change Framework—"C⁶"

As noted earlier, many firms are launching persistent (serial or overlapping) change initiatives in response to stressors in the environment. Clearly, one way to reduce the negative effects of *enervative change* (Dool, 2007) is to reduce the number of change initiatives launched by the organization. If recent history is a guide, this seems unlikely. The systemic impatience between organizational leaders and their stakeholders as well as the volatility in the environment indicates depending on a reduction in change initiatives is not a reasonable position. It would certainly help and should be encouraged, but another approach will also need to be pursued.

One of the challenges to the interpretation of the theoretical change models is that it is often assumed by practitioners that a "one-size-fits-all" approach. This is unrealistic. Change may have many common characteristics, but in practice, change is a situational and a specific experience for employees. Change management programs seem to be most effective when they are firm specific. Therefore, the new offering suggested here is a "framework," not a specific model. It is meant as a means to "frame" organizational strategies, processes, and tactics, in order to improve the organization's flexibility, agility, and to reduce the stress related to change.

It is proposed that this new change management framework, the "**C⁶**" framework, developed largely from the lessons learned from adaptive organizations, be deployed as a means to moderate the stress related to organizational change.

The C^6 framework is developed around six sets of leadership competencies: communications, collaboration, confidence, cohesion, climate, and conversion.

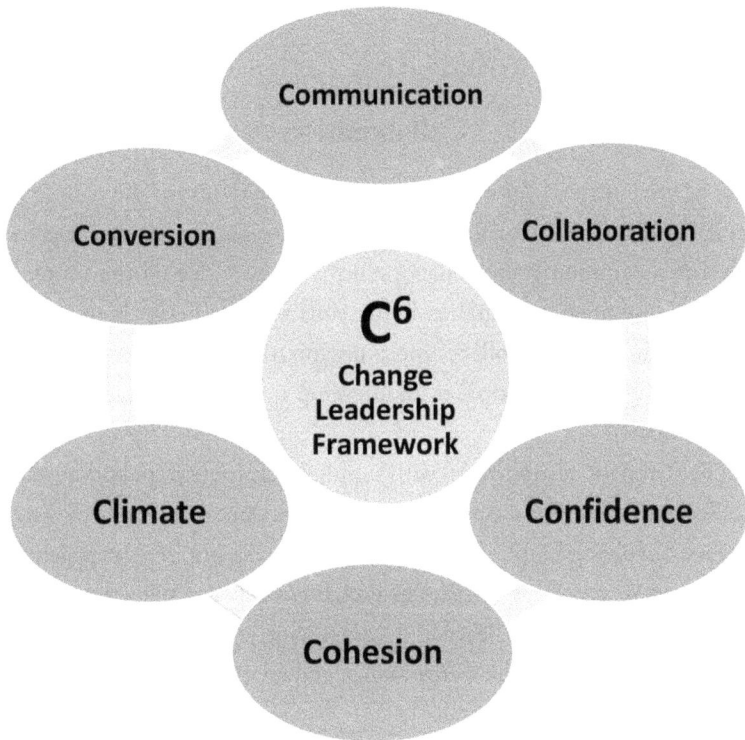

The C^6 framework is not intended to dictate a specific approach to change management.

It is being offered as a means for leaders to create firm-specific change management approaches enabled with practices related to the 6 "Cs." The specific purpose of the framework is to help reduce employee stress and ultimately infuse adaptability into the organizational DNA. Employees learn to be more resilient and reframe change cognitively into a "natural" organizational process.

Communication

The first element, *communications*, is of primary importance in reframing change. Leaders have learned that the effective flow of timely information serves to fuel adaptability. If employees understand the context, relationships, strategy, and tactical needs, they are better prepared to adapt to changes in the environment on a real or near real time basis. It has been found that 50 percent of failures are related in some form to ineffective communication (PMI, 2013).

Collaboration

The next element, *collaboration*, is also very important to the concept of "adapt and survive." Collaboration is the act of people working together to reach a common goal. Collaboration is the way that all the people in an enterprise function together. Better collaboration means better operations. With improved collaboration, organizations can increase the scale and capacity of their processes and develop new ways of doing business (Cisco, 2012).

The need for collaboration with suppliers, customers, and other stakeholders is essential for the organization to seize opportunities or to thwart threats. Involving employees early in the process improves engagement and broadens the scope of relevant exchanges between management and employees. Leaders have learned that involving employees in tactical discussions can improve unit performance and adaptability without undermining the chain of command.

Confidence

The next element, *confidence*, serves to build employee resiliency. Leaders must adopt an attitude of confidence in order to help manage employee stress during times of change. Wanberg and Banas (2000) found that optimism and perceived control were associated with openness to change. Change-related confidence is an important buffer against workplace stressors (Wanberg and Banas, 2000). An employee with a high level of self-efficacy is confident of "dealing with unexpected events, stays calm in the midst of difficulties and is able to handle whatever comes his or her way" (Tiong, 2005, p. 30). Confidence also comes with experience. Lau et al. (2002) note that people with more change experiences and more freedom to change will have a more positive outlook on about change. The more informed and prepared employees are, the more resilient and adaptable they become.

Cohesion

The next element, *cohesion*, is all about organizational identification. A high level of organizational cohesion improves morale and communication, builds resiliency and improves adaptability. Members of the organization take pride in membership and form strong bonds with their peers. Puuva and Tolvanen (2006) note that organization identity, when realized by organization members, has an effect on how strongly individuals within the organization identify themselves with the organization. Therefore, a strong identification results in the level of trust and in that way creates stronger commitment to the organization and its goals. Resilience refers to the ability to cope with ongoing disruptive change, bounce back easily from setbacks, overcome adversities, change to a new way of working and living when an old way is no longer possible, and do all this without acting in a dysfunctional or harmful manner.

Climate

The next element, *climate*, refers to the overall organizational environment created by managers. A positive, forward-facing, adaptive climate is more likely to reduce the debilitating aspects of stress related to change. Walsh et al. (2012) note "Climate" is people's perceptions and feelings about their work environment. Many leaders confuse climate with culture, thinking the climate cannot be controlled because it is too big and engrained in the organization. An environment of open-communications fostering the meaningful exchange of timely and appropriate information will improve decision making and adaptability. An environment that appreciates initiative, prefers to learn versus blame, and promotes organizational membership will likely increase the resiliency of its members.

Conversion

The final element, *conversion* refers to the ability of leaders to embed and sustain change, to convert the necessary adaptations into the natural DNA of the organization. Given the failure rates of change initiatives, as noted earlier, it is critical that leaders increase the probability that change initiatives will reach the expected outcomes, especially given the impact on precious resources. As Palmer et al. (2009) note, for change to "stick" it must be "become the new normality."

To be sustained, we must move from seeing change as a noun as noted earlier or an event, it must be seen as normal and not "change" with the baggage that traditional comes with the term (e.g., emotional, political, and negative connotations). There are a series of actions the effective change leader can take to embed or convert change into sustainable processes. These include: redesigning internal systems (e.g., reward, promotion, and recognition), redesigning roles, and linking decisions and behaviors to change objectives. Leaders should not expect change to be embedded by a conversion experience that focuses on attitude and beliefs, to be fully converted, they must change the employee's day-to-day experiences.

It is important to conversion that the change initiative be seen as working. There is always some doubt initially, especially given the high failure rates. Using appropriate metrics to track progress can serve several important functions. It can create positive momentum, it can offer "proof" to the naysayers or doubters that the initiative may indeed work, it can serve as an early warning system that something is off track and allow for proactive intervention, and finally, it can fuel interim opportunities for recognition and celebration that will add to the momentum.

It is also critical to conversion that employees up and down the organization "own" the change. This means they must "buy-in" to the change vision and also feel some responsibility for the expected outcomes. This can be accomplished in several ways including early and meaningful participation in the development of the change vision. A meaningful level of responsibility and accountability for the change initiative's success is also critical, giving the employees a "voice" in the actual implementation plan.

As noted earlier, the C^6 framework is not intended to dictate a specific approach to change leadership. It is meant to use lessons from the adaptive enterprise to promote the creation of an organizational environment that will foster adaptability as a means to reduce the negative impact of serial or ill-defined changes. The specific purpose of the framework is to infuse adaptability into the organizational DNA. Leaders will need to adapt and tailor this framework to the situation they face and the organization's culture, assets, and competencies.

Summary

The C^6 framework is not intended to dictate a specific approach to change leadership. It is meant to use lessons from the adaptive enterprise to promote the creation of an organizational environment that will foster adaptability as a means to reduce the negative impact of serial or ill-defined changes. The "C^6" change management framework has been offered as a means for leaders to create firm-specific change leadership approaches enabled with practices related to the 6 "Cs." The specific purpose of the framework is to infuse adaptability into the organizational DNA. Leaders will need to adapt and tailor this framework to the situation they face and the organization's culture, assets, and competencies.

Key Takeaways

- Change is a leader-led process, it demands consistent and persistent leadership intervention.
- Change is not likely to slow down in our working lifetimes.
- Leaders must be effective change agents, living and leading change by embedding it into the organizational DNA.
- Leaders need to reframe change from a noun to a verb, making it a natural part of daily organizational life.
- Leaders have to be the source of urgency as well as the source of psychological safety during change.

References

Agarwal, P. 2019. "Here Is Why Grit Is So Important for Entrepreneurs." https://www.forbes.com/sites/pragyaagarwaleurope/2019/02/17/here-is-why-grit-is-so-important-for-entrepreneurs/#ecbc1c151ddd, (accessed March 14, 2020).

Alton, L. 2018. "Workplace Changes Are Accelerating." https://www.forbes.com/sites/larryalton/2018/02/01/workplace-changes-are-accelerating-why-and-what-millennials-should-do-about-it/#439360d22def, (accessed March 21, 2020).

Anand, N., and J. Barsoux. 2017. "What Everyone Gets Wrong About Change Management." https://hbr.org/2017/11/what-everyone-gets-wrong-about-change-management, (accessed March 7, 2020).

Anthony, S. 2018. "6 Drivers of Change." https://hbr.org/2008/04/6-drivers-of-change, (accessed March 24, 2020).

Asher, P. 2018. "The Truth behind Why 70% of Organizational Change Projects Are Still Failing." https://www.imaworldwide.com/blog/the-truth-behind-why-70-of-organizational-change-projects-are-still-failing, (accessed March 8, 2020).

Baumgartner, N. 2019. "Change Is the New Normal: How to Build a Resilient Workplace." https://www.forbes.com/sites/forbeshumanresourcescouncil/2019/03/22/change-is-the-new-normal-how-to-build-a-resilient-workplace/#ba3bd975fc20, (accessed March 19, 2020).

Bruce, J. 2018. "Change Is the New Normal." https://www.forbes.com/sites/janbruce/2018/09/05/change-is-the-new-normal-how-will-you-handle-it/#180fa26e3959, (accessed March 17, 2020).

Center for Creative Leadership. n.d. "How to be a Successful Change Leader." https://www.ccl.org/articles/leading-effectively-articles/successful-change-leader/, (accessed March 17, 2020).

Cisco. 2012. "Creating a Collaborative Enterprise." http://www.cisco.com, (accessed August 5, 2012).

Dickson, G. 2019. "10 Reasons the Change Management Process Fails (and How You Can Succeed)." https://www.workzone.com/blog/10-reasons-the-change-management-process-fails-and-how-you-can-succeed/, (accessed March 12, 2020).

Dool, R. 2007. *Enervative Change.* Berlin: VDM Verlag Dr. Muller.

Elle, L. 2017. "Keeping Up with the World's Accelerating Rate of Change." https://pdcboston.org/ezine/keeping-worlds-accelerating-rate-change/, (accessed March 15, 2020).

Gleeson, B. 2017. "1 Reason Why Most Change Management Efforts Fai." https://www.forbes.com/sites/brentgleeson/2017/07/25/1-reason-why-most-change-management-efforts-fail/#1220f3c4546b, (accessed March 3, 2020).

Irwin, L. 2017. "6 Threats all Organizations Need to Plan for." https://www.itgovernance.co.uk/blog/6-threats-all-organisations-need-to-plan-for, (accessed March 13, 2020).

Kotter, J. 1996. *Leading Change.* Cambridge: Harvard Business School Press.

Lambertson, S. 2018. "Change Management: Understanding the Type and Drivers of Change." https://cloud4good.com/announcements/change-management-understanding-the-type-and-drivers-of-change/, (accessed March 22, 2020).

Lewin, K. 1947. "Frontiers in Group Dynamics: I. Concept, Method and Reality in Social Sciences; Social Equilibria and Social Change." *Human Relations* 1, pp. 5-41.

Lyteson, M. 2016. "7 Adaptive Enterprise Qualities." https://www.cio.com/article/3049970/7-adaptive-enterprise-qualities.html, (accessed March 21, 2020).

Mann, A. 2017. "Why Rate of Change Should Be the Most Important Metric in Your Company." https://www.cio.com/article/3219129/why-rate-of-change-should-be-the-most-important-metric-in-your-company.html, (accessed March 14, 2020).

Mingardon, S., M. Wolfgang, M. Lewis, A. Snyder, and G. Meyding. 2018. "Is Your Change Management Approach Keeping Pace with Digital?" https://www.bcg.com/en-us/capabilities/change-management/is-your-change-management-approach-keeping-pace-with-digital.aspx, (accessed March 20, 2020).

Murray, S. 2019. "Is 'AQ' More Important than Intelligence?" https://www.bbc.com/worklife/article/20191106-is-aq-more-important-than-intelligence?_lrsc=5cd072a9-8c3e-47e7-b334-d3fdd78bb12f&/?extcmp=soclie, (accessed May 5, 2020).

Ouye, J. 2011. "Five Trends That Are Dramatically Changing Work and the Workplace." *Knoll Workplace Research.* https://www.knoll.com/

document/1352940439324/WP_FiveTrends.pdf, (accessed March 14, 2020).

Palmer, I., and R. Dunford. 2002. "Who Says Change Can Be Managed? Positions, Perspectives and Problematics." *Strategic Change* 11, no. 5, pp. 243-51.

Palmer, I., R. Dunford, & G. Akin. 2009. *Managing Organizational Change: A Multiple Perspectives Approach.* New York, NY: McGraw-Hill Irwin.

Paredes, D. 2019. "Rapid Pace of Change Is Now Top 'Emerging' Business Risk: Survey." https://www.cio.com/article/3509788/rapid-pace-of-change-is-now-top-emerging-business-risk-survey.html, (accessed March 17, 2020).

Pendleton, H. n.d. "The Pace of Change, Part 1: Warp Speed Ahead." https://www.strong-bridge-envision.com/the-pace-of-change-part-1-warp-speed-ahead/, (accessed March 21, 2020).

PMI. 2013. "The High Cost of Low Performance: The Essential Role of Communications." https://www.pmi.org/-/media/pmi/documents/public/pdf/learning/thought-leadership/pulse/the-essential-role-of-communications.pdf, (accessed March 29, 2020).

Puuva, A. and U. Tolvanen. 2006. "Organizational Identity and Trust." *Electronic Journal of Business Ethics and Organization Studies* 11, no. 2, pp. 29-33.

Schein, E., and P. Schein. 2016. *Organizational Culture and Leadership.* 5th ed. Hoboken, NJ: John Wiley & Sons.

Sikora, P., E. Beaty, and J. Forward. 2004. "Updating Theory on Organizational Stress: The Asynchronous Multiple Overlapping Change (AMOC) Model of Workplace Stress." *Human Resource Development Review* 3, no. 1, pp. 3-35.

Smith, S. 2018. "The Biggest Threats to Your Business." https://www.forbes.com/sites/forbescommunicationscouncil/2018/02/26/the-biggest-threats-to-your-business/#5d7de4a14b85, (accessed March 15, 2020).

Tiong, T. 2005. "Maximizing Human Resource Potential in the Midst of Organizational Change." *Singapore Management Review* 27, no. 2, pp. 25-36.

Tucker, R. 2019. "Six Driving Forces of Change That Will Shape 2019 and Beyond." https://www.forbes.com/sites/robertbtucker/2019/01/25/six-driving-forces-of-change-that-will-shape-2019-and-beyond/#75c7d5de107a, (accessed March 29, 2020).

Walkme. 2020. "The Five Types of Organizational Change." https://blog.walkme.com/5-types-of-organizational-change/#1-organization-wide-change, (accessed March 5, 2020).

Walsh, B. M., V. J. Magley, K. A. Davies-Schrils, M. D. Marmet, D.W. Reeves, and J.A. Gallus. 2012. "Assessing Work Group Norms for Civility: Development of the Civility Norms Questionnaire-Brief." *Journal of Business and Psychology* 27, no. 4, pp. 407-20.

Wanberg, C., and J. Banas. 2000. "Predictors and Outcomes of Openness to Changes in a Reorganizing Workplace." *Journal of Applied Psychology* 85, no. 1, pp. 132-42.

World Economic Forum. n.d. "Drivers of Change." https://reports.weforum.org/future-of-jobs-2016/drivers-of-change/, (accessed March 29, 2020).

CHAPTER 8

Leader as Connector

Hanin Sukayri and Alcillena Wilson-Matteis

I start where the last man left off.

Thomas Edison

Introduction

A leader as a connector can be defined as a leader who knows how to connect with people and create relationships that can be leveraged to achieve the vision of an organization. They network to connect people who would benefit from working together. This leadership style fosters an environment that is best for collaboration, formally and informally, uniting different groups of people under a common goal.

There is no doubt that there is immense importance in the ability to network for one to be successful in any profession or field. Therefore, being a leader as a connector and being able to create and nurture connections, both internally and externally, will contribute to the whole team's success. To gain a complete perspective of this leadership trait, it is important to look at the acumen in both a historical and present-day context. We will explore how it has evolved and what we must do to adapt to the overwhelming velocity that we live in today. We will also explore the considerations and prerequisites a leader must have or achieve in order to be a successful leader as a connector. Throughout this chapter we will discuss key factors such as humility, psychological safety, and reflect on how this may cumulatively help enrich the leader as a connector.

The Importance of Networking

Connectors naturally network with people and organizations; however, all networking is not created equal. Networking is admittedly difficult, yet it can be done with the right mindset and role model. Networking is a prerequisite for transitioning from a manager role into a leadership position. Networking requires work and time in addition to your current role. According to Ibarra and Hunter (2019), "the alternative to networking is to fail—either in reaching for a leadership position or in succeeding at it." In fact, how you connect with your team as a manager is quite different from how you network and connect as a leader. "Effective leaders learn to employ networks for strategic purposes" (Ibarra and Hunter, 2019).

They observe networking as follows:

> In the process, we've found that networking—creating a fabric of personal contacts who will provide support, feedback, insight, resources, and information—is simultaneously one of the most self-evident and one of the most dreaded developmental challenges that aspiring leaders must address. (Ibarra and Hunter, 2019)

Additionally, they explain three types of networking and the most effective for the success of individuals, teams, and the organization:

1. Operational—Assists in managing day-to-day responsibilities
2. Personal—Boosts personal development
3. Strategic—Opens their eyes to new business directions and the stakeholders they would need to enlist

These three types of networks are not mutually exclusive and the most effective is strategic networking. However, incorporating all three network strategies will benefit an individual as he or she works on the goal of becoming a leader as a connector.

There are several ways in which a leader can create these networks. First, leverage each of the networks and find outside guidance and counsel to help navigate the transition. Connect with a person outside the organization, gain perspective, and learn new leadership styles. Allocate time to gather information from informal sources and think about how to use it to achieve goals. Stick with networking as you accomplish goals. Networking is an ongoing effort where "aspiring leaders must learn to build and use strategic networks that cross organizational and functional boundaries, and then link them up in novel and innovative ways" (Ibarra and Hunter, 2019).

Being a Connector 10 Years Ago versus Today

Twentieth-century leadership in organizations leaned toward the authoritarian and was often seen as demanding and intimidating. This top-down model was governed by rules and procedures and included climbing a social ladder for prestige, money, and power. By the end of the twentieth century, in addition to hierarchical structures, organizational leadership underwent a transformation as technology changed and advanced society into rapid instability (Agarwal et al., 2011, p. 632). Organizational leaders sought profits resulting in increased corruption at the start of the twenty-first century. Examples include the unethical practices of Enron leaders in 2001, to the subprime mortgage crisis of 2007, with leaders in various industries that contributed to failed banks and mortgage delinquencies and foreclosures. As a result of this poor leadership infused with technological advances, by the 2010s, organizational collapses and/or corporate scandals led people to lose trust in businesses. Companies were using old models and methods to function in a time when technology changed cultural norms in organizations and in society.

In the twenty-first century, hierarchical leadership does not work as well. The importance of being a connector started to emerge as the interaction of people and organizations on social media became a powerful tool impacting both organizational and personal lives in a myriad of ways. As one Silicon Valley CEO told me: "There is absolutely nothing wrong with command and control. It's simply irrelevant in the twenty-first century." The new leadership is a blending of personal and interpersonal skills that form the basis of your ability to impact, influence, and inspire others" (Goman, 2017).

From 1997 to 2007, a leader as a connector was one of the attributes attached to emerging leadership styles such as the "authentic leader" or "transformational leader" (Sayyadi, 2019). Research has discovered that the collaborative connector leadership style allows innovation to flourish through connecting individuals, teams, and organizations. Collaborative connector behavior includes silo-busting, building trust, aligning body language, promoting diversity, sharpening soft skills, and creating psychological safety (Goman, 2017).

Leaders Connect Things, People, and Organizations

The connector leadership style has traits and behaviors that influence the individual, the team, and the organization. The connector has positive assumptions about people and focuses on developing their talents. Either the connector assists employees in developing their talents or can connect them to those who can. In other words, connectors are self-aware of their skills and allow their teams to be trained by others who are experts in something that they are not. The connector values quality over quantity, for example, in conducting a team meeting, connectors advise what the meeting is for, why there is a meeting, and then encourage a high level of interaction. Leaders as connectors give specific or personalized feedback directly and tend to directly and confidently communicate tough issues. Connectors can talk one-on-one and with teams. They also help colleagues coach one another and connect with colleagues across the organization. Connectors do not necessarily have large networks, rather they are intentional and resourceful about who they are connected with in the first place (Ringel, 2014).

Individual Connection

Connectors are particularly adept with one-on-one interactions because they focus on the quality of the interaction. They ask the individual targeted questions and spend more time with employees than other managers, assessing the skills, needs, and interests of their employees. They talk less and listen more. They stay in the moment, making the most of every interaction. They also observe and recognize that people other than themselves may have valuable input. It is important to note that research shows that more time spent does not necessarily mean greater performance, it is more so about the tactics that connectors adopt in meetings that contribute to their success with individuals. In an interview on her research, Wilde observed:

> People come in with a lot of different skillsets and a lot of times, in most organizations, those are not used and so the manager in the team connection, the connector identifies individual differences. They're really good at embracing those, pulling those apart. They're known to create a more inclusive team environment so that people feel respected and comfortable sharing their individual skills with one another. (Wilde, 2019)

Wilde studied more than 5,000 managers to determine the different types of leadership styles. She observed that the connector's leadership style recognized a subordinate's skills, embraced their differences thereby creating belongingness, and used their uniqueness to contribute to and add value to the team. These three attributes are paramount in the connector's seeing an individual and the value they contribute.

Team Connection

Connections propel a team forward. The connector intuitively knows this and creates a sense of belonging within the team and organization.

Connectors embrace team differences thus creating a more inclusive culture where people feel respected and comfortable to share their individual ideas.

According to Ross (2017):

> Neuroscience experiments show that when people intentionally build social ties at work, their performance improves. Those that have high trust levels in the workplace have more meaningful relationships and feel both, secure in and loyal, to their group. They also know they have support when they need it.

The building of social ties at work increases progress and work productivity. It allows leaders to be open to work on other projects because they trust their team members to achieve excellence. In fact, when teams operate feeling connected to each other, the interaction is visible in the lunchroom. Ross (2017) provides eights tips for leaders to increase connection:

1. Regular productive meetings. As a 2015 study conducted on 2.5 million manager-led teams across 195 countries has shown, the engagement of the workforce was enhanced when supervisors practiced daily communication with their employees/staff members.
2. Share information widely. Share where the company is headed and why; sharing company goals, strategies, and tactics. Also, encouraging team members to share their knowledge builds connection and meaning.
3. Expressing gratitude at work. Leaders thank team members for their contribution and foster environments where team members thank each other. For example, you may have a gratitude ritual in the weekly meetings. Fredrickson's (2009) found that high-performance teams gave five positive comments to every one negative (5:1), while average teams had a ratio of 3:1.
4. Be a connector. High-stake leaders have successfully formed a high-stake network of peers and professionals that enable them to find the right people in any high stakes project. According to Logan (2008), high trust leaders create triads. They include three people (or more) in all their meetings. This reduces their time repeating

instructions, but it also builds trust, as everyone knows what is going on. Also, leaders you should help newcomers by removing common roadblocks; help them access information faster and whom they need to connect to and when.

5. Management by walking around. Increasing visibility gets people to review their work and leads to improvement. Increasing visibility makes people more likely to trust you.

6. Delegate work. It is more effective to delegate work because leaders get more done and direct reports feel good because they are being trusted to deliver.

7. Encourage cross-functional collaboration. This is to make sure individuals are highly networked. It can function in three ways: A. To solve a problem; B. Encourage learning about different departments; C. Promote individuals to meet with others in the organization or meet customers who benefit from their work. The best way to create cross-functional collaboration is to make it a ritual or a part of the organization's fabric.

8. It's party time! Celebrate accomplished work goals, milestones, and looking out for customers. Give teams time to socialize and talk about things that are nontask related. Sponsor lunches, dinners, activities, and after-work parties.

As can be seen above, the connector's leadership style itself is actually listed as a tip, further emphasizing the importance of a leader's collaborative effort. The cross-functional collaboration tip encourages individuals to learn from team members and/or from departments throughout the organization. This reveals how connector leaders are great at assembling teams and orchestrating positive environments. The connector's team goal is to develop an innovative organizational culture. A leader as a connector's mindset should be that it is not about me it is about the whole system.

Organizational Connection

A senior executive team's attitude toward making and maintaining intra-organizational connections will have a direct effect on how connections are made and sustained by staff at-large (Rosenberg, 2020). This is particularly relevant when it comes to companies and organizations that have multiple subcompanies, locations, and/or divisions that are physically and culturally separated. In fact, a leader for a multinational company must embody an attitude of creating formal, informal, and interpersonal networks, thereby becoming familiar with how each division operates. "Through songs, picnics, and fun sporting events, employees can feel a sense of togetherness," all of which comes from an effort to connect seemingly disparate parts of an organization (Lee, 2013).

How Do Executive Connectors Create a Connected Culture?

Stallard offers three core elements that leaders must keep in mind when going about the process of connecting their organization (Trapp, 2015). He had other building blocks for connectedness, but vision, value, and voice were core components of connection. He describes them as follows.

1. A *vision* must be able to be used to motivate people to do what is important. You can do this by having a clear phrase that describes the vision, mission, and values that employees understand.
2. *Value* is helping people find roles that fit their interests and provide mentorship and training plays an important part in creating connection cultures.
3. *Voice* is about creating a flow of knowledge that produces shared understanding between the leader and the led. It is vital however that the leader is seen listening to others' views before making choices.

We discussed how connectors bridge together things, people, teams, and organizations. We then examined how connectors operate within each connection. The connector's actions overlapped or were intertwined. It all begins with the connector's characteristics and how it is used in interacting with individuals, teams or the organization connector.

In our analysis, we suggest one begins to implement the above actions within their business. First, embrace individual differences and their skills and interests that they bring to the table. Next, encourage teams to communicate by conducting intentional strategic actions like weekly meetings, and allow members to be heard; and team members should be coached to teach each other. In the organization, create a sense of belonging by including differences within the organization's culture and use this action step of inclusivity to build a community within the business, which will impact business beyond the organization. Thus, create greater work satisfaction within the company and greater business growth.

Summary

Through considering the comparison between a leader as a connector in the present and historically, and realizing the importance of networking, there are many factors that a leader as a connector must take into consideration. A leader as a connector must be mindful of all that their team is exposed to in order to gain a better understanding of how they would best connect and collaborate to deliver the most viable and successful results possible. Being cognizant of their level of humility, what they do in the workplace to foster psychological safety and as a whole, how they act as leaders is paramount to the success of their leadership as connectors.

Connectors form strategic networks, give feedback, and are resourceful in tailoring skills or interests to develop individuals, teams, or the organization within and outside of the corporation accomplishing the best outcomes of the goals set. Networking is a cyclical give-and-take of actions that builds trust and fosters innovation for business growth. The hierarchical leadership of the twentieth century has transformed into soft skills of self-awareness, authenticity, and the valuing of differences in the twenty-first century. This soft-skill leadership approach is in direct connection with the knowledge economy that is influenced by the rapidness of social media impacting both organizational and personal lives in a myriad of ways. The connectors value individuals, and this builds strong teams that aid in positive organizational culture and innovation. The organizational culture starts from the one-on-one interactions, to team collaborations, finally positively impacting the whole organization's functions.

Key Takeaways

- It is paramount for a leader as connector to have humility.
- A leader as a connector must ensure psychological safety in the workplace.
- A leader as a connector is strategic about network implementation.
- Leaders embrace differences and leverages them to achieve goals.
- A connector communicates frequently in these rapid times (i.e., organized weekly meetings).
- Everyone feels a sense of belonging and their contributions are utilized.

References

Agarwal, R., S.L. Johnson, and H.C. Lucas. 2011. "Leadership in the Face of Technological Discontinuities: The Transformation of EarthColor." *Communications of the Association for Information Systems* 29, pp. 627-44. doi:10.17705/1cais.02933.

Fredrickson, B. (2009). *Positivity*. New York, NY: Crown Publishing Group (Three Rivers Press)

Goman, C.K. July 11, 2017. "Six Crucial Behaviors of Collaborative Leaders." https://www.forbes.com/sites/carolkinseygoman/2017/07/11/six-crucial-behaviors-of-collaborative-leaders/#6e1c30fb8cbe, (accessed April 25, 2020).

Ibarra, H., and M.L. Hunter. February 7, 2019. "How Leaders Create and Use Networks." https://hbr.org/2007/01/how-leaders-create-and-use-networks, (accessed May 18, 2020).

Lee, S.J. 2013. "How Does an International Company Ensure That Its Culture Remains Intact While Also Be Flexible Enough to Cater to Local Behaviors?" https://digitalcommons.ilr.cornell.edu/student/23/, (accessed March 25, 2020).

Logan, D., King, J., & H. Fischer-Wright. 2008. *Tribal Leadership: Leveraging Natural Groups to Build a Thriving Organization.* New York, NY: HarperCollins Publishers.

Ringel, J. April 28, 2014. "How to Build Your Network Like a Super Connector." https://www.entrepreneur.com/article/233429, (accessed April 19, 2020).

Rosenberg, M. January 29, 2020. "Ways Leadership Affects Culture and Culture Affects Leadership." https://www.hrexchangenetwork.com/hr-talent-management/columns/ways-leadership-affects-culture-and-culture-affect, (accessed May 15, 2020).

Ross, M.C. (November 12, 2017). "8 Tips for Leaders to Increase Connection in their Teams (Part 3)." https://trustologie.com.au/2017/11/12/8-tips-for-leaders-to-increase-connection-in-their-teams/, (accessed April 12, 2020).

Sayyadi, M. March 21, 2019. "How Transformational Leadership Harnesses the Power of Knowledge." https://blog.hrps.org/blogpost/How-Transformational-Leadership-Harnesses-the-Power-of-Knowledge%C2%A0, (accessed March 11, 2020).

Trapp, R. May 27, 2015. "Why Successful Leadership Depends On Connections." https://www.forbes.com/sites/rogertrapp/2015/05/26/why-successful-leadership-depends-on-connections/#434e8fe822ba, (accessed February 25, 2020).

Wilde, S. November 12, 2019. "Why 'Connector' Managers Build Better Talent [Audio Podcast]." https://hbr.org/podcast/2019/11/why-connector-managers-build-better-talent.

CHAPTER 9

Leader as Talent Manager

Tahsin Alam and Saumil Joshi

I am convinced that nothing we do is more important than hiring and developing people. At the end of the day, you bet on people not on strategies.

Lawrence Bossidy

Introduction

The days of leaving talent recruitment, retention, and professional development to the human resources offices down the long hallway are quickly disappearing. As we enter a time with multiple generations in the workplace, a gig economy, and a workforce eager to be connected to the leader of an organization and/or team, living in the speed of now necessitates that a leader not only be present, but proactively participate in securing, retaining, and developing talent. While history may dictate that we look to someone's past experiences as evidence of future success, today applicable transferable skills, as well as cultural fit, are quickly becoming equally, if not more important (Rouen, 2011).

Today, in order to be a leader as talent manager, three distinct skill sets are needed: developing an ability to identify the talent needs of an organization and establish a firm recruitment process to secure the talent, being involved in the development and implementation of strong retention policies and practices, and finally, being invested in the professional growth of your employees (Miles LeHane Companies, Inc., n.d.).

Given the competitive nature of the labor force, and with the increase in attention given to skill sets rather than exclusively years of experience, a leader's ability to recognize and acquire talent will make or break an organization's growth trajectory (Cohn, 2014). The war for talent is severe and will only grow in the coming decades. As the variety and choices of jobs and careers increase, workers will embark upon multiple careers in their lifetime (Keller and Meaney, n.d.). Today's 20-somethings may work for 8–12 firms in a 30+year working career. According to the United States Bureau of Labor Statistics, the average tenure of workers is 4.2 years as of January 2018, which is notably less than a decade prior (US Bureau of Labor Statistics, 2018). A leader's participation in the recruitment process shows a dedication to the workforce that could set an organization apart from other competitors. For example, today's organizations are in a race for acquiring, manipulating, and utilizing data to make informed decisions (Singh, 2018). In this context, for example, hiring talented data engineers and data analysts has become a talent arms race. What is particularly interesting about data professionals is that they are somewhat agnostic to the actual subject matter for which the data is being utilized. Simply put, data analysts are the chameleons of industries today, able to move from an engineering company to a software company to a non-profit while utilizing the same value-added skills. As a result, a leader will likely be interviewing a data analyst who has a multitude of employment options and offers available to them. If a candidate choosing between three jobs has met the leader of either the team or the entire organization through the interview process, it will leave an indelible impression that will help that organization stand out over the competitors where the leaders have not made the time to meet with the candidate. So, in recruiting, participatory leadership has now become critical, especially as the war for talent rages. In the future, it would not be surprising if leaders spend the majority of their time doing recruitment and increasing their social media presence in order to build a brand that can attract quality candidates. As tenure continues to drop, recruitment and talent scouting will become near an ongoing role for a leader, particularly given the expectation by candidates to see a participatory leader during the hiring process.

Given this global economy, it would be a mistake for today's leaders to consider talent management as a competency that is limited only to the recruitment process. Today's leader will need to be able to identify varying and evolving skill sets in their existing workforce in order to identify translatable skills in other areas. They also have to be willing to find talent from nontraditional sources and in different "packages." Often companies have the traditional or standard sources for talent recruitment (e.g., competitors). In the future, they will need to extend their sources to ancillary sources or even unexpected sources in the search for talent. They also will need to consider candidates that may not have the traditional profile and search for those with aligned skills, but also may bring other competencies or experiences. For example, Richard Branson of the Virgin Group is known for moving his successful employees to different areas of his organization, regardless of their history and background with regard to work (Henry, 2018). Brett Godfrey, originally the CFO of Virgin Atlantic relocated to Australia and pitched the idea of building and serving as the CEO of Virgin Australia to Branson. While Godfrey had never served as a chief executive officer, Branson trusted Godfrey with the task and provided all the capital that was needed to build what is now one of Australia's most successful airline carriers (Aim, 2014).

Retention strategies are an equal partner to recruitment in this competitive landscape. Earlier this decade, retention was becoming misunderstood as perks, (i.e., providing ping-pong tables, volleyball courts, free food, etc. similar to those amenities found at Google offices) became in vogue (Vasel, 2018). Whether that directly contributed to retention is hotly debated; however, what is very clear in today's workforce is that employees want to see two things: learning opportunities and professional development and growth (Zappe, 2019). A leader involved in talent scouting must also be directly involved in talent retention. Organizations without a learning platform, professional development opportunities, and a clearly articulated career growth trajectory for its employees will lose the talent arms race, even if they have the best recruiting platform available. Today's leader needs to contend with the mindset of today's worker and understand fully what motivates the talent to stay in the organization. The ability to understand this, provide such programs, and be involved in evolving these programs over time will become a critical part of a leader's success.

Talent Recruitment—The Nuts, Bolts, and Strategy

Often referred to as talent acquisition, the recruitment of talent starts with properly identifying your organization's talent needs followed by finding a way to articulate these needs and recruiting the right people (Lybrand, 2018). Proper identification of the talent needs at hand ensures that everybody, the leader, and the team, are all on the same page as to the needs and skill sets for the vacancy or new position. Without knowing what you need to hire, it is hard to figure out whom to recruit and that increases the likelihood of making an incorrect hire. Further, not having clearly articulated expectations for the position and the new hire will not position the person for success (Heathfield, 2019). As sometimes can be the case, companies scramble to fill vacant positions without proper attention to exact needs, cultural fit, and overall integration with the team. Embarking on an exercise where all these details can be ironed out with an intent to hold the position accountable to success, will ensure that in the medium and long term, the overall team and/or organization will be successful. This is true in any industry. Whether it is the hiring of the right drivers for a Formula One team, identifying the right set of skills for an engineering team, or bringing in a specialized set of skills to a medical practice, agreement on the needs of the position is crucial (Cappelli, 2019).

Internal Talent Identification

The recruitment process, in broad terms, can take two forms. Some organizations, typically larger and well-resourced ones, will develop their own recruitment teams and processes. For example, most major banks have substantial recruitment teams for any position from entry-level all the way to just below the executive (Noel, 2014). A leader needs to be able to assemble a recruiting team and point them in the direction of where the greatest strategic talent needs are for business. In a growing business, a recruitment team will continuously play catch up to fill all the positions needed. But having an internal recruiting team allows for economies of scale where networking becomes a professional expectation and deliverable. The more these internal recruiters are networking in the same space, the more they will know whom to attract. The efficacy of the team, however, depends entirely on the team or company leader providing clear direction on priorities.

Outsourcing Recruitment

The outsourced recruiting industry (i.e., recruiting firms that will help you hire the talent that you need) is a large industry in the United States and poised to continue growing (Joshi, 2020). Recruiting firms will specialize by industry and by position level. Some firms are specialized in technology, banking, pharmaceuticals, etc. while either at the same time or separately, specializing in entry to mid-level positions or strictly for executive positions. These companies are continuously recruiting and as such will provide significant value added to a leader who decides to take this route. With that said, you are less likely to experience the aforementioned economies of scale by using search firms, primarily because they have competing interests with other clients looking for the same talent. Further, this is a very expensive option, but may be the only option for smaller companies. The right mix of using internal recruitment and external recruitment, interspersed with passive recruitment—posting jobs and seeing what comes in—is up to the leader of the organization to prescribe in today's high labor demand marketplace.

Retention Efforts

Recruitment of talent will feel like a never-ending, thankless effort if not immediately followed by comprehensive retention efforts. In the competitive landscape of today, leaders putting effort only in recruitment, but not in understanding the mindset of the workforce and what keeps them motivated and staying happy in their jobs will result in an effective brain drain of the individuals who have been recruited (Syed, 2017). This is the proverbial other side of the coin; other companies will inevitably take on aggressive recruitment efforts to recruit away your own hard-fought talent. The only real and strategic solution or defense to this competitive landscape is to have strong, deeply personalized retention efforts to keep your talent. To do so requires keeping one's finger on the pulse of what workers and employees across industries are looking for in the workplace. For example, some easy to answer retention solutions include providing your workforce with the appropriate technology needed to do their job, proper training for your managers so that they manage appropriately and fairly, multicultural sensitivity training since the modern workforce is quickly diversifying and, particularly in the United States context, respectable benefits for all workers. On the latter point, the next level up would be to analyze additional benefits such as extended parental leave above and beyond federal FMLA standards, the option of telecommuting, which is becoming an increasing requirement of many early career professionals and ongoing training and education benefits (Jones, 2017). Many organizations have gone even beyond these measures, as in the case of the Bill and Melinda Gates Foundation, wherein recent years they have adopted unlimited vacation days and providing a stipend to any employee with children (Gillett, 2015). Larger companies such as Goldman Sachs also offer paid childcare as well as many other conveniences for young families. A large part of this stems from the significantly increasing percentage of female workers in the workforce, the source of which can be traced to the massive increase in female college graduates (Flaherty, 2018). All signs show that these demographic changes will continue, and as such, and astute the leader will need to adapt and execute these new retention efforts to keep their players.

A major part of retention today also involves culture. First, while anecdotally leaders might think that the current generation of workers is not interested in being held accountable, evidence shows that workers today need direction and communication of expectations followed by timely and frequent feedback (Tandon, 2019). Secondly, much like creating a culture of feedback, developing an overall inclusive, transparent, communicative, and accessible workplace are all things that today's talent looks for during the interview stage of any job search (Lever, 2020).

Substantial research supports that nowadays individuals will leave a job, not because of salary as the primary driver, but rather poor management and a lack of a transparency culture (Schwantes, 2020). Setting the tone for the culture, expending resources to build and sustain the culture, and maintaining a competitive position are all responsibilities of a leader in today's organizations.

Professional Development

As covered in this book's "leader as mentor" chapter, employees today are seeking direction and mentorship for their career and future aspirations. As such, a discussion on talent management is a trait that is critical to a leader's role as a mentor. In this chapter, however, professional development is referred to as a macro level responsibility of a leader. Much like retention strategies, to which professional development is inextricably connected, today's leader must invest in overall professional guidance, investment, and growth for all employees in an organization. Today's workers are looking for a clear path forward, or at a minimum, a clear understanding of what growth potential there will be in an organization. Workers will quickly feel like they are in a dead-end job if leadership has not articulated a future for them connected to the future of the company. There are multiple solutions that can be enacted, all of which however stem from a leader's investment in an overall professional development structure. In the past, such options were limited to executives or those further up in the organization. Today, sustaining these privileges only for long-term or senior employees will bring on increased turnover rates and an unsupported culture, both of which are a slippery slope toward low-quality talent acquisition.

Key Attributes of a Leader as Talent Manager

For a leader to embody, put into practice and provide a vision for managing talent in an organization or team, we view the following attributes and responsibilities as critical to developing a leader's talent management competency. While there are a variety of ways in which one can develop a talent leader, these attributes provide a comprehensive answer to how talent acquisition, retention, and professional development can be developed in the hands of a leader operating at the speed of now.

Participatory Leadership in Recruitment

To put it simply, the presence of an organizational or team leader in the interview process for hiring a team member cannot be understated. Evidence shows that candidates are far more likely to accept a job where they have had the opportunity to meet with either the team leader or the company leader overall (Cohen, 2019). Too often, leaders leave this assignment to human resources or other members of the team, particularly when it is not a direct report. Stephen Starr, the leading restaurant owner in Philadelphia with additional restaurants in New York City and Florida, totaling over 30 total restaurants, is well known for interviewing every single hire at every location. Be it servers, hosts, or managers, Starr understands that his is a people-based business and people are the basis of his success (McGrath, 2018).

Critically important in this equation, however, is that a leader also understands how to sell. Often, leaders tend to think of an interview as one sided: the interviewee needs to impress the interviewer alone (Prescott and Cross, 2009). In today's economy, a leader's inability to capture the imagination of the interviewee, express the organization's vision and direction, and inspire excitement will result in losing leading talent. Even if a leader is not extroverted, learning how to create a two-way conversation during an interview and being able to articulate his or her vision is a critical aspect of securing the best talent in the market.

An extension of a leader's ability to sell his or her vision includes being ready to assist hiring managers or human resources in "dislodging" a hard to get candidate. As discussed later, the best companies will take on proactive recruitment and identify candidates who are perfectly happy in their current jobs. To bring the right talent to the organization, the leader needs to be ready to go the extra mile and that they should be bringing their talents to his or her company. Some high-value candidates need convincing to even attend an interview. A successful leader as a talent manager will see this as an opportunity rather than a reason to claim that will he or she should not need to convince anyone to interview.

Talent-Centric Mindset

Today's companies that embed continuous talent identification and nurturing across the entire organization are those that are able to attract and keep the best talent (Pandit, 2007). It is critically important for a leader to build a culture where every manager sees it is their responsibility to continuously work and recruit the best people. Furthermore, a recruitment-minded culture unpaired with clearly articulated standards of performance and success could result in an organization hungry for talent but without quality standards. As such, a leader will need to articulate on a regular basis the importance of performance, values, and hiring standards.

To that end, companies today are very quickly heading toward skills and values-based interviewing rather than a history of experience alone. In our high technology world, companies, organizations, and online hiring websites are beginning to put a higher premium on skill set over educational pedigree and immediately applicable job history (Yoh, 2019).

Sharon Koifman, founder and CEO of DistantJob, a recruiting firm specializing in placing virtual employee, and an expert in global recruitment, agrees that "With the rapid advancement of technology and the rise of highly specialized technology-related jobs, it's safe to say that the IT and tech fields are in much greater need of a strong talent acquisition strategy than other fields" (Jobvite, 2017).

As hiring trends in the twenty-first century evolve, we will begin to see a greater degree of tools and measures to identify the strength of skills. As such, it is incumbent on a leader to begin the mind shift away from looking at talent as strictly a historical valuation, and more based on transferable skills. For example, excellent management skills can translate and transcend industries particularly if the demands of the role are to manage a large group of employees. If an engineering company looking to hire a strong manager does not consider a very strong manager from a pharmaceutical background simply based on subject matter expertise, the engineering company, in the long run, is likely to lose out on the talent needed to succeed. Such skills-based identification of candidates is also a guaranteed way of identifying nontraditional candidates as well as diverse individuals. The job history-based type of interviewing and candidate selection can sometimes be inadvertently exclusionary or limited to only the background of individuals. As such, looking more widely at skills will allow a leader to diversify the workforce both in terms of racial, gender, and age diversity just as much as diversity of thought (McConnell, 2019).

All of the above, though, is predicated on embracing a more proactive recruitment strategy. Leaders of today need to embrace the idea that proactively identifying candidates that fit the company's needs is going to win more often than lose in the talent war. Whether that is done by outsourcing to search firms or in-sourcing with dedicated recruiters, in today's LinkedIn era, almost anyone can do the research needed to identify candidates with the proper fit of skills and background. To win the talent battle of the future, leaders today need to start thinking research and proactive outreach when it comes to filling key vacancies.

Cultural Transformation

Setting an organization's mission, vision, and values and disseminating it across the organization is critical for a myriad of reasons, all closely studied and supported in research and case studies. But the importance of mission, vision, and values bears to be repeated when it comes to talent recruitment and retention. Today's workers, especially early career professionals, are attracted to organizations that have mission focus and a value system (Pandologic, 2015). As mentioned above, a leader needs to be ready to articulate the vision, mission, and values during an interview. As such, a part of a leader as talent manager involves ensuring that this vision, mission, and values are not only internal anchors of culture, but also an external representation of what it would be like to work at that company.

A very close partner to developing and evangelizing vision, mission, and values internally in an organization is the leader's disposition and embodiment of transparent and accessible leadership. Woven in with being available for talent interviews is the need for a leader to be transparent and accessible to new hires. Developing a culture where your employees can reach and speak to leaders across the organization will substantially increase retention rates across an organization (Erickson, 2015). While this might be difficult for the leader of a very large company, creating a transparent and accessible culture will result in others within the organization embracing the same attitude. Given that many workers nowadays have begun to rank leadership access as a top reason for staying with a company, a leader's role as talent manager must include setting an example of leadership that attracts the best talent from the marketplace.

Tangible Benefits for the Modern Workplace

Technology today is allowing workforces to be more and more mobile. While some industries such as agriculture, manufacturing, grocery stores, etc. involve hands-on work to run the business, most other businesses, particularly those that are technology-heavy, are capable of allowing their workers to work from just about anywhere (Vize, 2018). Today's leaders need to understand with this convenience comes an increase in new hires wanting to take advantage of telecommuting and flexible work arrangements. In particular, early career professionals are increasingly seeing this benefit as an expectation rather than a perk. Companies conducting work capable of being done remotely who do not have any telecommuting policy will most certainly risk attracting and retaining the best talent for their business. It is incumbent on the leader to provide or advocate for flexible work arrangements, even if it is limited. Soon companies without flexible work will be seen as outdated and unattractive by the growing workforce. Kathleen Quinn Votaw, the founder and CEO of TalenTrust states, "I advise clients and executives to Always Be Cultivating by thinking of recruitment as a sales process. If you want A-players on your team, your company must spend as much time and effort attracting and retaining employees as it does on finding and keeping customers" (Jobvite, 2017).

In close connection with the above is a leader's responsibility to ensure that, with available resources, the workforce is equipped with as good technology as affordable to the company. Companies can sometimes overlook the importance of technology as a recruitment and retention tool. Top talent attracted to a company who subsequently is frustrated by the lack of technological utilities will quickly find a new place to go (Rayome, 2019). At the same time, this point should not be overstated. A leader must balance the technological needs of the workforce with the realities of budget. But to that degree, a true leader as a talent manager will continuously advocate for the most affordable and best technology for the workforce, not just for the sake of productivity but also for the purposes of recruitment and retention will.

With no intention of wading into the political, it is important here to discuss the need for companies to examine their paternal benefits. As previously discussed, the workforce continues to diversify, particularly with an increase in female employees in the workforce. At the same time, there are more dual-income households today than ever before (Miura and Higashi, 2017). From a purely talent management point of view, companies with enhanced paternal leave options will attract more of this changing workforce and keep them for longer. As such, in the discussion of a leader being a talent manager, this topic that holds an incredible amount of decision power for top-performing talent must be considered in order to stay competitive in today's talent market. There is a multitude of options: from increasing paid leave, to allowing flexible use of leaving the dates, providing a one-time stipend for child care costs, to as much as providing paid child care on an ongoing basis, companies today are adapting to this reality. Such companies are also able to develop a family-oriented culture, which is increasingly important to today's workforce. Simply put, only doing the federally required minimum will hurt companies more than doing just a little more.

Social Media and Corporate Branding

Companies and organizations today all have a certain degree of social media and public marketing plans in place, if for no other reason than to promote their product or service. Today's leader must take into account how social media and online presence now equates to a brand image that talent will gravitate toward, or in the absence of an internal cultural brand identity, will gravitate away from. We previously discussed the importance of the mission, vision, and values of the organization. In the current talent market, it is equally important to display and organization's vision, mission, and values in action on public social media platforms. This gives top talent and insight into the working culture, a top decision maker for accepting or rejecting a job today (Duce, 2019). Workers today spend a significant amount of time doing online research of potential employers before or during an interview process. It is in effect a two-way street: as much as candidates need to impress the potential employer, candidates need to be impressed by what the employer has to offer based on publicly available information. It is incumbent on a leader today to have a substantial marketing strategy in place in order to secure the best talent possible.

In fact, one of the most powerful ways in which to communicate this is by having the leader themselves embrace a social media presence. Sara Blakely, founder and CEO of Spanx, fully embraced as this tactic by openly talking about her personal struggles as a leader and due to motherhood and her belief system on how to run a company (Dool, 2019). In so doing, Blakely gave the public an insight into her leadership style, her humanity, and the culture of the company. Marketing like this cannot be underscored enough—leaders willing to be open, vulnerable, and strategic in sharing information about themselves and their company culture will invariably attract not only top talent but a talent that is preselected itself to having a belief system similar to that of the company.

Succession Planning and Internal Pipeline Growth

Over the past decade succession planning has been considered an important part of any major business or organization. While there are plentiful ways in which this can be done, it is quite surprising to see a number of organizations that do not have a succession plan in place beyond only the CEO (Bernier, 2015). What this creates is an environment of uncertainty for other leaders within an organization. Today's leaders must institute succession planning and high potential analyses throughout the organization, if not for the majority of positions, then most certainly for business-critical roles. Once again, in the context of talent recruitment and retention, workers today will look for succession planning from the outside and expect to follow through on the inside. A leader's ability to create, roll out, and execute these plans will increase both their ability to bring in top talent and to keep them.

Similarly, while a succession planning tends to be relegated to senior and key positions, creating career ladders for every level of position starting from entry-level roles will further enhance a company's ability to attract and retain talent. In particular, organizations that have clear steps of progression throughout the organization tend to be more successful in sustaining motivation and keeping career-driven individuals (Kemelgor and Meek, 2008). In fact, an astute talent manager will make time to have one-on-one career discussions with direct reports as well as skip meetings with employees further down the chain of command. This marries nicely with the points made above about transparency, staying involved in career growth and developing a culture that is attractive to today's workers. Furthermore, a leader must play the part of cheerleader, where they celebrate career progression within the organization and publicly acknowledge growth within the organization. This is critically important because existing employees want to be valued as much as incoming employees.

Leader as Talent Manager: A Checklist

To provide a starting point, the following is a checklist of actions traits and behaviors that a leader can embody to develop a culture and organization reflective of the points made above:

Participatory leadership in recruitment	Make yourself available for as many interviews in your organization as possible. Select key positions based on importance but also on distance for your role.
	Create a "sell sheet" of how to talk about the company and/or team with interviewees. Practice to make perfect.
	To get the best talent, be ready to make a hard sell, go above and beyond. Fight for the best talent.
Talent-centric mindset	Encourage other team members to always be on the lookout for talent. Read "leader as mentor" chapter for additional guidance.
	Articulate and evangelize standards of hire.
	Embrace skills-based interviewing instead of only job history as a means of measuring potential.
	Encourage a higher proportion of proactive, targeted hiring rather than a passive job posting.
Cultural Transformation	Socialize your organization's mission, vision, values as a yardstick for identifying talent.
	Internally evangelize standards of performance so that managers know the standards expected of new hires.
	Embrace transparent and accessible leadership.

Tangible benefits for the modern workplace	Champion flexible work and telecommuting if possible for your business.
	Conduct a technology review to identify gaps so that competitors do not have an edge with talent attraction.
	If you have not already, begin discussions on how to provide supplementary benefits to workers with children and dual-income households.
Social media and corporate branding	Work with your marketing team to develop an attractive, consistent, people-centric social media window into your company's values and inner workings.
	Develop your own social media presence, prepare to share more about yourself, your value system, and your leadership style. Read "leader as ambassador" chapter for further guidance.
	Encourage employees to do the same so that they too can become ambassadors for the organization.
Succession planning and internal pipeline growth	Develop a clear succession plan for yourself and senior members of the organization.
	Create career ladders for all classes of employees.
	Celebrate, publicly, internal promotions and take on one-on-one annual career discussions with a direct report and skip reports.

Summary

For a leader to be successful as a top manager, they must undertake both aspects of internal transformation, outlook on talent acquisition and retention while also undertaking some very tangible changes to their organization. While automation and artificial intelligence may threaten many classes of jobs in the future, just as many if not more jobs will remain in the workforce for the foreseeable future. With that in mind, of course, every job will be hotly contested and the arms race for talent will continue to elevate. Leaders without both a personal and practical outlook on recruiting and retaining talent will lose out in this battle if they do not take proactive measures immediately. As online job boards and websites continue to proliferate, the market is constantly leveling the playing field for companies in attracting top talent. Therefore, the leader of today and the future will need to continuously be on the cutting edge of what makes them, their company, and their culture competitively different from others. The measures and changes in outlook outlined in this chapter, whether taken in pieces or completely, will begin to give you an edge on the competition.

Key Takeaways

- Being a talent manager today requires participatory leadership in the full cycle of recruitment, retention, and talent development. Workers today expect to see and interact with leaders in each of these steps.
- The hiring world is quickly moving to a skills-based hiring model rather than one simply based on work experience and history. Today's leader will need to make this pivot as soon as possible.
- Investing in workplace culture is just as important as the effort to hire top talent. Studies have shown that culture and management practices are the leading reason that workers stay with an employer.
- Leaders must invest in their personal presence in social media and branding. Personal brand along with advertising workplace culture will attract talent away from other opportunities.

References

Aim. 2014. "Brett Godfrey's Hands-on Strategy Helps Virgin Take Off." http://blog.aim.com.au/brett-godfreys-hands-on-strategy-helps-virgin-take-off/, (accessed April 26, 2020).

Bernier, L. 2015. "Succession Planning Not Just About CEO (Executive Series)." https://www.hrreporter.com/news/hr-news/succession-planning-not-just-about-ceo-executive-series/281191, (accessed March 22, 2020).

Cappelli, P. 2019. "Your Approach to Hiring Is All Wrong." https://hbr.org/2019/05/recruiting, (accessed February 15, 2020).

Cohen, P. 2019. "New Evidence of Age Bias in Hiring, and a Push to Fight It." https://www.nytimes.com/2019/06/07/business/economy/age-discrimination-jobs-hiring.html, (accessed April 2, 2020).

Cohn, C. 2014. "Why You Should Hire for Core Skills Rather Than Experience." https://www.forbes.com/sites/chuckcohn/2014/09/08/why-you-should-hire-for-core-skills-rather-than-experience/#27ab4b9a15bd, (accessed March 17, 2020).

Dool, R. 2019. *12 Months of Leadership Insights*. 1st ed. Seattle, WA: Amazon.

Duce, J. 2019. "StackPath." https://www.industryweek.com/talent/article/22027154/better-recruiting-through-social-media, (accessed April 3, 2020).

Erickson, R.A. 2015. "Communication and Employee Retention." *The International Encyclopedia of Interpersonal Communication*, pp. 1-10. doi:10.1002/9781118540190.wbeic239.

Flaherty, C. 2018. "New Analysis Suggests Women's Success in STEM Ph.D. Programs Has Much." https://www.insidehighered.com/news/2018/09/18/new-analysis-suggests-womens-success-stem-phd-programs-has-much-do-having-female, (accessed April 7, 2020).

Gillett, R. 2015. "Bill Gates Is Now Offering His Foundation Employees a Full Year of Paid Parental Leave." https://www.businessinsider.com/gates-foundation-announces-unlimited-leave-policies-2015-10?international=true&r=US&IR=T, (accessed April 8, 2020).

Heathfield, S. 2019. "What's the Big Deal about Clear Performance Expectations?" https://www.thebalancecareers.com/what-s-the-big-deal-about-clear-performance-expectations-1919253, (accessed April 11, 2020).

Henry, A.E. 2018. *Understanding Strategic Management*. 3rd ed. https://global.oup.com/academic/product/understanding-strategic-management-9780199662470?cc=us&lang=en&#.

Jobvite. 2017. "What Is the Difference between Recruitment and Talent Acquisition?" https://www.jobvite.com/recruiting-process/what-is-the-difference-between-recruitment-and-talent-acquisition/, (accessed April 13, 2020).

Jones, K. 2017. "The Most Desirable Employee Benefits." https://hbr.org/2017/02/the-most-desirable-employee-benefits, (accessed April 12, 2020).

Joshi, S. 2020. "Recruitment Process Outsourcing Market Expected to Reach US\$ 40.67 Bn by 2027 with a CAGR of 29.1%." https://www.einpresswire.com/article/506760255/recruitment-process-outsourcing-market-expected-to-reach-us-40-67-bn-by-2027-with-a-cagr-of-29-1, (accessed April 4, 2020).

Keller, S., & M. Meaney. n.d. "Attracting and Retaining the Right Talent." https://www.mckinsey.com/business-functions/organization/our-insights/attracting-and-retaining-the-right-talent

Kemelgor, B., and W. Meek. 2008. "Employee Retention in Growth-Oriented Entrepreneurial Firms: An Exploratory Study." *Journal of Small Business Strategy* 19. https://www.researchgate.net/publication/267779005_Employee_Retention_in_Growth-Oriented_Entrepreneurial_Firms_An_Exploratory_Study.

Lever. 2020. "8 Things Candidates Want from Employers in 2020." https://www.lever.co/blog/8-things-candidates-want-from-employers-in-2020/, (accessed April 26, 2020).

Lybrand, S. 2018. "What Is Talent Acquisition and How to Do It." https://business.linkedin.com/talent-solutions/blog/recruiting-tips/2018/what-is-talent-acquisition, (accessed April 10, 2020).

McConnell, B. 2019. "12 Ways to Improve Your Diversity Recruiting Strategy," *Recruitee Blog*. https://blog.recruitee.com/diversity-recruiting-strategy/, (accessed April 14, 2020).

McGrath, T. 2018. "Stephen Starr on Creativity and Listening to Your Instincts." https://www.phillymag.com/business/2018/10/27/stephen-starr-restaurateur/, (accessed April 15, 2020).

Miles LeHane Companies, Inc. n.d. "The Ultimate Guide to Recruiting & Retaining Top Talent." https://www.mileslehane.com/recruiting-retaining-top-talent#final_thoughts, (accessed April 17, 2020).

Miura, K., and M. Higashi. 2017. "The Recent Increase in Dual-Income Households and Its Impact on Consumption Expenditure." https://ideas.repec.org/p/boj/bojrev/rev17e07.html, (accessed April 16, 2020).

Noel, J.S. 2014. "The State of Talent Acquisition and Management in Banking and Financial Services UK." https://recruitingblogs.com/profiles/blogs/the-state-of-talent-acquisition-and-management-in-banking-and, (accessed April 19, 2020).

Pandit, Y. 2007. "Talent Retention Strategies in a Competitive Environment." *NHRD Network Journal* 1, no. 3, pp. 27–29. doi:10.1177/0974173920070307.

Rayome, A.D. 2019. "Would You Quit Your Job Over Bad Software? 24% of Employees Have Considered It." https://www.techrepublic .com/article/would-you-quit-your-job-over-bad-software-24-of-employees-have-considered-it/, (accessed April 21, 2020).

Rouen, E. 2011. "Is It Better to Hire for Cultural Fit Over Experience?" https://fortune.com/2011/04/28/is-it-better-to-hire-for-cultural-fit-over-experience/, (accessed April 22, 2020).

Schwantes, M. 2020. "Why Do People Quit Their Jobs, Exactly? It Comes Down to 3 Reasons, According to Research." https://www .inc.com/marcel-schwantes/why-do-people-quit-their-jobs-exactly-it-comes-down-to-3-reasons-according-to-research.html, (accessed April 23, 2020).

Singh, H. 2018. "Using Analytics for Better Decision-Making." https:// towardsdatascience.com/using-analytics-for-better-decision-making-ce4f92c4a025, (accessed April 24, 2020).

Syed, S. 2017. "Stop the Brain Drain: 4 Ways to Keep Your Employees Engaged." https://www.cmswire.com/digital-workplace/stop-the-brain-drain-4-ways-to-keep-your-employees-engaged/, (accessed April 3, 2020).

Tandon, R. 2019. "Periodical Feedback Helps Identifying Consistent Performers across Verticals." http://bwpeople.businessworld.in/article/ Periodical-Feedback-Helps-Identifying-Consistent-Performers-Across-Verticals/30-04-2019-169946/, (accessed April 1, 2020).

US Bureau of Labor Statistics. 2018. "Employee Tenure Summary." https://www.bls.gov/news.release/tenure.nr0.htm, (accessed April 25, 2020).

Vasel, K. 2018. "Why Perks Aren't the Answer to Employee Retention Problems." https://edition.cnn.com/2018/09/30/success/perks-employee-retention/index.html, (accessed April 14, 2020).

Vize, S. 2018. "Why Remote Work Is the Future of IT & Tech." https:// www.mondo.com/remote-work-future-of-tech/, (accessed April 5, 2020).

Yoh. 2019. "In Absence of a Perfect Candidate, 75% of Americans Would Most Likely Choose Soft Skills Over Experience and

Qualifications When Making a Hire, Yoh Survey Reveals." https://
www.globenewswire.com/news-release/2019/03/05/1747934/0/en/
In-Absence-of-a-Perfect-Candidate-75-of-Americans-Would-Most-
Likely-Choose-Soft-Skills-Over-Experience-and-Qualifications-
When-Making-a-Hire-Yoh-Survey-Reveals.html, (accessed April 6,
2020).

Zappe, J. 2019. "Employees Want to Grow Their Career So How Are You
Helping Them?" https://www.tlnt.com/employees-want-to-grow-their-
career-so-how-are-you-helping-them/, (accessed April 25, 2020).

CHAPTER 10

Leader as Coach and Mentor

Lloyd Pearson and Ngwa Numfor

Mentoring is not only a fantastic way to build your own leadership capabilities, it's a way to give back.

Julian Carle (2018)

Introduction

A leader's primary responsibility is to help those around them reach their full potential (Truter, 2008). This makes the leader as a coach and as a mentor a vital competency for leading in today's workplace. A team needs a leader who can be versatile by leading their colleagues effectively and properly developing them in their roles.

There has been a plethora of research (Carle, 2018; Truter, 2008; Kouzes et al., 2010) outlining benefits of employing leadership competencies such as coaching and mentoring.

In order to do this, it is important to differentiate the roles of the two competencies and note where they differ and how they overlap. It is also important then to examine ways in which a leader can develop the competency. While developing this competency, establishing clear principles on aspects to avoid or implement is crucial.

Employees today do not want to be micromanaged. They want to be led in a more indirect style with leaders using coaching, mentoring, suggesting, and through the creative use of questions. This allows employees to solve problems themselves and gain crucial experience in order to improve their careers. Employees want to be more directly involved, feel valued, have a voice, and feel like a unique member of the team (Randel et al., 2018, p. 192). Ownership and trust increases team members' engagement and productivity. For this to occur, it is vital that leaders have an understanding of the coach and mentor leadership competencies, and how to apply them with their own teams.

The duality of leadership as a coach and mentor is akin to two sides of the same coin. A coach knows when to motivate and inspire. They are technical in their analysis and push their team to produce results to their maximum potential. They help define goals and manage expectations. Coaches hold everyone accountable, including themselves and understand how to manage each personality on the team. The approach as a coach is normally direct and is one that prioritizes performance and output.

A mentor is more of a guiding, perhaps even familial figure. They typically have more of a stake in the well-being and trajectory of a person overall. A mentor has strong prior knowledge and is especially sought out for this. Like a coach, a primary obligation of the mentor is to hold people accountable as well. They tell their mentees what they need to hear in a personalized and constructive manner. Mentors often represent a more holistic approach than a coach.

Upskill Consulting (n.d.) noted from Maya Angelou:

In order to be a mentor, and an effective one, one must care. You must care. You don't have to know how many square miles are in Idaho, you don't need to know what is the chemical makeup of chemistry, or of blood or water. Know what you know and care about the person, care about what you know and care about the person you're sharing with. Mentoring is not about being the best at everything. It is about using the knowledge you have acquired and sharing it with someone else in order to help them be successful. These relationships are based around a common goal. Through understanding what the mentor/mentee can attain from one another, it can help fuel their desire and become a more engaged worker.

They also quoted from Cagneey: "Coaches are aware of how to ignite passion and motivate people. They have an energy that is contagious and know exactly how to get their team excited."

The needs and the development of employees and those on one's team must be the main priority of both a coach and a mentor. A leader must be able to transition between coach and mentor roles depending on the situation at hand. Both coaches and mentors have a duty to those around them to stay engaged, dynamic, and ensure that everyone is developing.

Comparing and Analyzing Leader as Coach and Leader as Mentor

Jane (2020) offers this listing to highlight key elements of both roles:

Coaching and Mentoring – The Differences and Similarities

The following table identifies the differences and similarities between coaching and mentoring.

	COACHING	MENTORING
Focus	Receiving structured support to develop awareness and find own solutions	Giving instruction and direction
Context	Depends on how coaching is requested (i.e. team, individual or organisation)	Generally personal or professional development
Intention	Asking client questions and discovering a solution	Telling client solutions to their problem
Progress	Made by agreement at start of coaching	Made by agreement at start of mentoring
Expert in Content	Client	Mentor
Expert in Process	Coach	Mentor
Level of Accountability	Medium to high	Medium to high
Level of Sector Knowledge	Low to medium	Medium to High
Importance of the Client's Commitment	Very	Very
Main Professional Skills of Coach and Mentor	Listening, questioning, feedback, explicit goal setting, building trust and action planning	Listening, questioning, feedback, explicit goal setting, building trust and action planning
Content	Based on needs of the client	Based on needs of the mentee
Level of Formality	Formal – contract and ground rules set	Informal to formal – depends on intention
Level of Training for Coach or Mentor	Diploma (however depends on coach - good question to ask)	Depends on mentor (good question to ask)
Level of Contract	Typically between 4-12 meeting over 2-12 months	Typically unspecified number of meetings with relationships spanning 3-5 years
Number of Participants	Can be individual, team or organisational	Generally one-to-one

Maybe the difference can be summarised as follows:

"A coach has some great questions for your answers; a mentor has some great answers for your questions."

Truter (2008) offers these four key qualities for a Mentor:

Four Key Qualities of Mentors

Relevant work experience	This includes passing on experience and knowledge, how to best approach a task and where potential pitfalls lie.
Experience and knowledge of the organization	Knowing how to get things done and acting as a gateway to sources of information and support.
Interpersonal skills	Knowing how to listen, asking questions that are both challenging and reflective. It is this "sounding board" approach that is one of the most valuable aspects of mentoring and it is essential when getting a mentee to focus on their task (how to approach it generally and how to solve problems).
Role model	Providing an example that encourages, motivates, and reassures the mentee, making it clear that the task they are trying to achieve is attainable.

This quote from Truter (2008) further assists in encapsulating the nuances between the coaching and mentor leadership competencies:

The strength of mentoring lies in the mentor's specific knowledge and wisdom; in coaching it lies in the facilitation and development of personal qualities. The coach, in other words, brings different skills and experience and offers a fresh perspective—a different viewpoint and objectivity. In a mentoring relationship, both the mentor and the mentee may have a political stake in the relationship. In a coaching relationship, neither the coach nor the individual they are coaching needs the other. Their relationship is mutually enjoyable and results in the development and growth of both parties.

Competency in Action—Leader as Mentor

Mentor: Someone whose hindsight can become your foresight.

Anonymous

Implementing the GROW Model

One way in which leaders can utilize their own experience/expertise to help others is by putting goals and strategies into perspective. Carle (2018) recommends the GROW model. This will help the mentee during mentoring sessions, and the mentor to drive the sessions. The GROW model is a simple, but purposeful framework for structuring a mentoring session.

Goals	What does the mentee want to achieve?
	First, you and your mentee need to look at the behavior that you want to change, and then structure this change as a goal that the mentee wants to achieve.
	Make sure that this is a SMART goal: one that is Specific, Measurable, Attainable, Realistic, and Time bound.
Current reality	What are the current circumstances the mentee faces, in relation to the goals they have set?
	This is an important step. Too often, mentees try to solve a problem or reach a goal without fully considering the starting point, and often they're missing some information that they need in order to reach their goal effectively. They may be treating a symptom and not the actual root issue.
Options (or obstacles)	This is where the mentor uses their skills, experience, and expertise to assist the mentee in framing their options and how best to navigate them. It is imperative at this stage that the goals be completely the mentee's own.
Will (or way forward)	Finally, setting realistic milestones. What is to be done, with whom, and how? It is the mentor's responsibility to hold the mentee accountable over the course of the mentoring period.
	By examining the current reality and exploring the options, your mentee will now have a good idea of how they can achieve their goal.
	But in itself, this may not be enough. The final step is to get mentee to commit to specific actions in order to move forward toward the goal.

Approaches to Mentoring

Truter (2008) maintains that a leader must view mentoring and coaching from two perspectives. To provide leadership/mentorship/coaching to others, and to allow themselves to be given guidance. The importance of a learner having a mentor in some capacity is further reiterated by the Carle (2018) and Kleine (2003). Truter (2008) presents these mentoring approaches:

Informal mentoring	This occurs all the time and is an integral part of managing and leading people, whether planned or not. It occurs when trust is built up and a learner finds a more experienced colleague that they respect, trust, and feels they can learn from.
Role model	As a consequence of the mentoring process, the mentee will inevitably be influenced by the mentor's attitudes, values, problem-solving techniques, and people management skills.

(continued)

Sponsorship mentoring	Under this system the mentor provides a wide variety of experiences and opportunities for the mentee, usually through special projects and assignments. This system is particularly useful in large organizations that may want to "fast track" the development of key staff or groups.
Peer group mentoring	This system is most commonly used for new recruits joining an organization. It involves a responsible colleague at a similar level passing on their advice and help. It is an approach that works well as part of an induction process, and it is particularly useful for smaller organizations where training and development is achieved by using existing staff resources.

The following graphic illustrates practices to avoid and engage in for mentors: (Bowling Green State Provost, 2020).

Do's and Don'ts for Mentors and Mentees

What makes a good mentor?

What a mentor DOES

Listen: function as a sounding board for problems and ideas

Criticize constructively: point out areas that need improvement, always focusing on the mentee's behavior, never his/her character

Support and facilitate: provide networking experience, share knowledge of the system; offer assistance where needed

Teach by example: serve as a model for adhering to the highest values in every area of life

Encourage and motivate: help mentees to consistently move beyond their comfort zone

Promote independence: give their mentees every opportunity to learn by experience

Promote balance: serve as a model for balance between professional and personal needs and obligations

Take pride in the success of their mentees: recognize that students may rise to greater levels than those who trained them

What a mentor DOES NOT do

Protect from experience: do not assume the role of problem solver for the mentees

Take over: do not do what the mentees should be doing themselves

Force: do not attempt to force a mentee in one direction

Use undue influence: do not use a sense of obligation to influence the mentee's professional decisions

Lose critical oversight: do not allow friendship to shade over into favoritism

Condemn: do not convey to the mentees that honest mistakes are career-altering disasters

What makes a good mentee?

What a mentee DOES

Take the initiative: recognize the need for mentoring and seek it out

Avoid perfectionism: accept that you will make mistakes, and learn from them

Maintain balance: preserve time for family and friends

Work hard: are prepared to give your best

Support your peers: exchange personal and professional support with fellow trainees

What mentee DOES NOT do

Avoid difficulties: do not expect mentors to solve all your problems for you

Sidestep work: do not expect mentors to do work that you should be doing yourselves

Stay in your comfort zone: do not shy away from new learning experiences

Take advantage: do not use friendship with a mentor as a tool to avoid work or escape consequences of your own activities

Bottle it up: do not avoid talking about problems, anxieties, or grief because it makes you seem less than perfect

Competency in Action—Leader as Coach

Coaching is not about teaching the caterpillar how to fly, it's about creating an opening for it to see the possibility.

Paul Lefebvre

How a Leader Develops This Competency

Here are some practices or tools that may help enhance the coach competency (Morley, n.d.):

Practice	Meaning	Rationale
Ask, don't tell.	Instead of telling a team member what they did "wrong," ask them guided questions to show potential flaws.	This coaching practice allows the leader to remain humble in their approach and give the team member ownership of their own development.
Be empathetic.	Showing that the coaching stems from wanting to benefit the person being coached and improve their contributions to the team.	This practice is important to show team members that their leader is not blind to their efforts and their challenges.
Progress is success.	Focus on progress to keep motivation high.	Not every day will lead to tangible "successes."
Coach daily.	Structure coaching into your daily routine.	Coaching is intentional. Go into every interaction realizing there is a potential for improvement.

Summary

Today's leaders should not try to force the traditional rules of management on today's diverse workforce. They don't try forcing a fit for an employee. Instead, they actively seek out coaching and mentoring opportunities with employees to improve productivity, morale, and retention. As a leader in today's landscape, it is imperative to mentor (Carle, 2018) and implement coaching insights (Elcombe, 2017; Truter, 2008). Coaching, in simple terms, means to train, tutor, or give instruction. It is a critical skill that is used to enhance growth and performance, as well as promote individual responsibility and accountability. Coaching is a continuous process that builds and maintains effective leader–follower relationships. Mentoring and coaching are critical leadership and management competencies today. Employees are asking more and more for coaching.

Employees in today's professional landscape are not favorable toward micromanagement, favoring a more indirect, calm, and inclusive style (Randel et al., 2018, p. 192). These two aspects of leadership are two sides of the same coin, and equally important in leadership. Leaders need to inspire, nurture talent, helping those around them grow and learn. Through further development of coaching and mentoring competencies of leadership, one can expect to see positive growth for both mentors and mentees.

Key Takeaways

- The duality of leadership as a coach/mentor has become a critical competency, especially with the younger generations.
- Today's employees do not want to be directed, ordered, told, or micromanaged. They prefer the overall indirect style associated with coaching and mentoring.
- It has been shown that effective coaching and mentoring can have positive impacts on productivity, morale, resilience, and retention.
- The mentoring process, if done well, creates benefits for both the mentor and the mentee.
- Effective coaches not only accurately identify challenges; they are proficient at developing solutions.
- A mentor provides support for the employee, but the ultimate goal is to empower the employee to work independently with the skills they have learned.
- Forward thinking organizations blend both coaching and mentoring to develop strong and effective employees and also identifying future leaders to mentor.

References

Bowling Green State Provost. 2020. "Do's and Don'ts for Mentors and Mentees," *Bowling Green State University*. https://www.bgsu.edu/content/dam/BGSU/provost/center-undergraduate-research-scholarship/

documents/Dos-and-Don-ts-of-Montors-and-Mentees.pdf, (accessed April 12, 2020).

Carle, J. 2018. *Give Back, Lead Forward: Why Every Leader Should Be a Mentor and have a Mentor.* Highett, Australia: Major Street Publishing.

Elcombe, T. 2017. "Beyond 'Crude Pragmatism' in Sports Coaching: Insights from C.S. Peirce, William James, and John Dewey: A Commentary." *International Journal of Sports Science & Coaching* 12, no. 1, pp. 33-34. doi:10.1177/1747954116686176.

Jane. January 9, 2020. "Coaching and Mentoring—The Differences and Similarities." https://www.habitsforwellbeing.com/coaching-and-mentoring-the-differences-and-similarities/, (accessed May 19, 2020).

Kleine, K. 2003. *Becoming a Mentor Leader in a Professional Community.* Lanham, MD: Scarecrow Education.

Kouzes, J., B. Posner, and E. Biech. 2010. *A Coach's Guide to Developing Exemplary Leaders Making the Most of the Leadership Challenge and the Leadership Practices Inventory (LPI).* San Francisco, CA: Pfeiffer.

Morley, K. n.d. "Four Coaching Practices that Every Leader Should Master." https://www.iidmglobal.com/expert_talk/expert-talk-categories/leadership/coach_mentor/id114015-four-coaching-practices-that-every-leader-should-master.html#AuthorCredits, (accessed April 12, 2020).

Randel, A.E., B.M. Galvin, L.M. Shore, K.H. Ehrhart, B.G. Chung, M.A. Dean, and U. Kedharnath. 2018. "Inclusive Leadership: Realizing Positive Outcomes through Belongingness and Being Valued for Uniqueness." *Human Resource Management Review* 28, no. 2, pp. 190-203. doi:10.1016/j.hrmr.2017.07.002.

Truter, I. 2008. "Responsibilities of a Leader as Mentor and Coach." *Management* 75, no. 5, pp. 58-61.

Upskill Consulting. n.d. https://www.upskillconsulting.ca/2018/04/25/mentoring-and-coaching/, (accessed June 20, 2020).

CHAPTER 11

Leader as Producer

Natalie Spangenberg and Alissa Zarro

Effective leadership is not about making speeches or being liked; leadership is defined by results, not attributes.

Peter F. Drucker

Introduction

A leader as producer is a leader who executes on goals and objectives, drives tangible results, and utilizes feedback and experience to inform decisions about the process of reaching these objectives.

They are also responsible for the products and services they offer within their organization, including the quality. A producer is efficient and resourceful, knowing how to solve problems, which shows they are proactive in anticipating possible problems, managing conflicting priorities, and keeping a pulse on their team's needs. A good producer is also good at listening to feedback and possible problems from all stakeholders.

They delegate effectively to work out solutions that help meet or exceed end goals in a sustainable way.

Leaders today must be able to create a compelling vision and strategy, but they must also be able to deliver the expected outcomes. They have to seamlessly move between the strategic and the operational/tactical often on the same day. It is one thing to create the strategy; it is another to deliver (produce) it.

The following are key areas in order to be a good producer:

- Executing on goals, objectives, and driving tangible outcomes
- Being a responsible leader
- Driving efficiency, speed, and resourcefulness
- Knowing how to solve problems
- Managing and delegating effectively
- Analyzing critical data and information
- Being concerned about the process

Executing on Goals, Objectives, and Driving Tangible Outcomes

To be a producer, a leader not only visualizes the outcome, but sets it in motion through implementation and execution. It is important for a leader to be able to achieve results and deliver on the vision of the organization. Doing this will determine whether or not initiatives are successful, and what could be done differently in future endeavors. This will also help to understand the various variables of success and how to sustain them.

Being a Responsible Leader

Responsibility comes in many forms and variations when it comes to a leader. A producer is responsible for the products, service, and quality of their organization, as well as the day-to-day operations of the organization in which they lead. This includes being responsible for the work, but also the people of the organization—making sure operations are run effectively and problems are resolved efficiently and in a timely manner. Especially with how globalized the current workforce has become and continues to develop, leaders are responsible for being involved in what is happening within their organization, especially within the production processes that occur, regardless of location. A leader cannot be present in every location at once on a day-to-day basis, but they can still be present in the process in various ways that help to support and act upon the organization's goals and initiatives.

As stated in Dool (2019),

> A major transition among business leaders in the 21st century has been a widespread sense of acceptance that executives must answer not only to their own fiduciary interests, but to the long-term impact of the companies they run on the future of an increasingly globalized world.

Driving Efficiency, Speed, and Resourcefulness

A producer also needs to be efficient in the work they conduct, helping other members of their team be efficient in their work as well. This will help determine how fast a process is conducted and the resources needed to deliver on a goal or objective within an organization. Whether a leader as producer is the most senior executive, head of a department, or leader within a team, a producer is able to deliver in these areas to help drive success for their organization. This also includes being resourceful in who the leader selects to achieve various goals.

Being efficient in the work and having the proper resources in place will help speed up the time it takes to accomplish a goal, which will help to drive additional projects forward. Concurrently, with the pace of work, being able to handle multiple projects at once is another key area for a producer. They must be multifaceted and able to set priorities, but also dive into the details. Oftentimes, they will be handling more than one project that they are responsible for and must be able to see the whole picture, while also getting into the weeds at times on an individual project.

Knowing How to Solve Problems

In the midst of executing upon organizational goals and initiatives, a producer also knows how to address and mitigate problems as they occur. Not acknowledging these problems as they occur can affect not only processes, but how teams ultimately work, as well as the outcomes. A producer knows how to be proactive in managing conflict, and listening to teams about problems they may experience, as well as their needs in the midst of day-to-day operations. They know when to intervene and when to stand back. They understand when triaging is useful and when to rethink processes. They use data and instinct both to keep a pulse on the operations of the organization as well as an active monitoring process.

To be a good problem solver as a producer, it is important to listen to feedback from all parties involved and those a leader delegates to for input. They create active, bidirectional communication channels. A producer will work out solutions with their teams, which will drive to the end goal in a sustainable way. There will always be problems to solve and conflicting opinions or ideas, but these situations present an opportunity for the leader as producer to see what actions they can take to help drive operations forward in the best way possible. Founder, CEO, and president of Amazon, Jeffrey Bezos, has embodied success in a variety of ways, but has been active in being a problem solver in his leadership at Amazon. Dool (2019) mentions this by noting:

Be unmovable, but willing to give. This first strategy might seem a bit contradictory. How can you be stubborn and flexible at the same time? The answer is simple—stay focused on your business plans and goals, but be willing to make changes if necessary. A business leader that lacks the ability to be stubborn is likely to abandon plans instead of seeing them through, and a leader lacking flexibility may overlook finding solutions to problems. ... An industry inevitably will grow and change in ways that are hard to anticipate. To find success, stay true to the company's goals, but be willing to adapt plans as the industry evolves.

Managing and Delegating Effectively

There are two important aspects to being an effective leader as a producer. It's important to not only focus on the process from end-to-end, but also to properly manage teams in a way that guides them. Leaders set the goals, boundaries, and expectations and the rules of engagement as well as an effective monitoring process. They allow and encourage their teams to actively offer input on the work and their own ideas on the path to success. A producer has to have effective management skills that promote success for their teams. This includes ensuring team members are united under a common goal and communicating to keep teams informed and facilitating interdepartmental teamwork. It's crucial for a leader to be present and be a source of guidance for their teams while executing on goals and objectives of the overarching organization. Leaders as producers have to lay the foundation for their team members, especially when they are first starting out within an organization. A producer is good at delegating and communicating desired outcomes in a clear, understandable way. They facilitate an organizational environment where their teams feel confident to do the work they are responsible for completing, but also provide support in cases where a team member may need guidance.

As leaders continue to navigate the fast pace of society, where technology is integral to how the majority of work is being conducted, it's important to realize how teams will, in turn, form and operate available technology and systems. Leaders should be able to anticipate and incorporate new technology as seamlessly as possible into their employees' work.

Analyzing Critical Data and Information

With every action taken by an organization, there are opportunities to analyze the results and outcomes of those initiatives to see what worked, what didn't, and how every outcome can be used to grow and build for future initiatives. Even with initiatives that may appear to have "failed," there are always opportunities for growth and an opportunity to try again in the future, but in a different way. Even during the process of execution, a producer may learn new information or ideas that can possibly change an outcome and shift the course of that initiative as it is happening to change the direction.

In every stage of innovation and production, producers should be able to justify their results to ensure they correspond to the company's mission, purpose, and values. They have to put in place an active monitoring process that provides accurate and timely data on performance. This enables leaders to know when to intervene or stand back. They create meaningful metrics (e.g., key performance indicators (KPIs) or milestones) that can be used to track progress, serve as an early warning system, build momentum, serve as a reason to celebrate or offer proof to naysayers. This will have a direct impact on how employees help to produce in those key areas as well.

This is extremely important because the work being done within an organization should have a positive impact whenever possible. A producer keeps this in mind through focus and analysis, and executes on those fundamental areas that will drive success back to the organization and the work being done. This will also help to bring in more consumers who are buying in to what the organization stands for through their mission, purpose, and values, not to mention current and future team members who are passionate about what the organization stands for.

Being Concerned about the Process

In relation to the process of the work, a leader who is a successful producer also understands they have to lead in different stages of the production. When it comes to the process of the work, it's important for a strategy to be clearly defined. The tactics to deliver that strategy can be implemented to drive tangible and sustainable outcomes. A leader who produces decides on the responsible parties involved and their role within projects. It's also important for a leader to see a process from end-to-end, making sure their team members are driving results, and also that the processes are being executed in a sustainable manner. This will help to create a system of success by giving feedback where necessary and keep the team informed.

Zachary Langway, adjunct lecturer at Rutgers University and Towson University, (2020) notes,

> Leader as Producer means striking a balance of doing and motivating. To be a leader, you have to produce, to roll up your sleeves and get in the trenches with your team. But you also need to know where to step back and let your team get the work done—with your support and motivation, but trusting them to get the job done. So, it is about finding balance and looking for the ways you can contribute meaningfully and uniquely while at the same time, distributing tasks and empowering your team to be their best in achieving your shared objective.

How a Leader Develops This Competency

How to Execute on Goals, Objectives, and Drive Tangible Outcomes

A key element in how a leader develops and enhances the producer mindset is simply through continuous action. This will help to put production into perspective and lead to future actions being taken. A leader who is good at executing on their goals is also good at organizing and keeping track of many moving parts. This can be accomplished with good time management and organizational skills. Other ways this can be developed and enhanced is through meeting with teams and keeping track of the status of processes being executed. It's important, especially in the initial stages to be aware and present, but it's also important to be involved throughout the stages of production as they are happening to gain a sense of how things are going, how teams are doing, address any concerns or problems, and see the final outcome in sight even if it's not completely done yet. Again, it's important for a producer to be involved and play an active role, but to also provide the freedom for teams to grow and have their own opportunities to take an active role on what is being done.

Dool (2019) noted,

> Having a big picture perspective is great, but leaders cannot ignore the importance of the details. This balancing act is one of the biggest challenges professionals face as they advance in their careers. In the end, strategy is vital but worthless without execution.

How to be a Responsible Leader

Prior (2020) says that the lines are blurred between the roles and activities of being a producer, manager, and leader. She notes,

> The way to succeed is to let go of the idea that you play just one role, and that you'd be more effective if only you could delegate more effectively. Your lifeline is your ability to shift mindset and hold onto the idea that your job is now to simultaneously produce, manage and lead.

Oftentimes leaders fail when they take an approach of less day-to-day involvement. This can be detrimental to the work being done and the chemistry of a team. Leaders are responsible for not only being active in the production of the work, but also for being present for their teams. Being a leader, manager, and producer demands becoming more immersed at times with their teams, especially to communicate the team's purpose before execution, to drive success within organizations. The best leaders have an active monitoring process in place as noted earlier and use it to know when to intervene and when to stand back. They also know through intuition, honed by experience, that intervening both too early or too late can both have unintended consequences.

Leaders are responsible for each aspect of their business, and this includes not only team output, but product or services output. It is easy for leaders to become removed from things such as product quality and operations.

Indra Nooyi, former CEO of PepsiCo, has been an influential leader and embodies a true producer. She recognized the responsibility she had when running the company, and it has shown through the success of the PepsiCo business, which gives perspective to other leaders who are trying to be producers by recognizing the responsibility they have in their own organizations. Dool (2019) notes:

> She runs the company not only by looking at the big picture but she is also into details. Nooyi goes to stores and checks how their products are doing, from how they are displayed on shelves to the print quality of the logos. If she sees not enough products are catered to a particular market in a location or demographic, she takes note of this and does something about it.

How to Manage and Delegate Effectively

Kanaga and Prestridge (2002) noted:

> One of the first steps to take toward increasing team effectiveness is to pay attention to how the team is formed. You can head off most of the problems that beset teams during the formation

stage by setting a clear direction, securing organizational support, selecting the right team members, building an enabling team design, developing key relations, and monitoring external factors.

Dool (2019) also goes into depth about how leaders can encompass key managerial skills:

A leader needs to identify the key players who can make a project succeed and then offer them the resources to push the project forward. Empowering a small group of talented individuals to work together increases the chances of identifying ideas that help the business innovate.

Good managerial skills include knowing how and when to delegate. This involves recognizing your employees' strengths and giving them roles that allow them to act on them, giving good directions, and resolving any confusion regarding an individual's roles and responsibilities in order to have a clear understanding of what is expected. It is paramount to highlight and document the most important points and aspects decided on so that everyone can refer back to them and be on the same page.

To develop this competency of being a producer, it's a unique blend in taking the active steps in executing on the process, but still giving freedom to the teams to actively work as well. It's also taking an active role in what strategies are being implemented. As a leader, it's important to be involved, but also be aware of your role within teams and projects that are being implemented and adapted where necessary. Therefore, practicing a balance between micro- and macro-managing can help give freedom to organizational teams, and also allow a leader to be there if needed and provide support and guidance throughout. Dool (2019) also adds:

Successful leaders know how to define their mission, convey it to their subordinates, and ensure they have the right tools and training needed to get the job done.

An important way to be a good manager is keeping an open dialogue with subordinate members of the team. These lines of communication may be formal, in the form of meetings, or they may be informal conversations. The best leaders create both formal and informal, active bidirectional communication mechanisms that provide critical information, but also what they need to hear versus want to hear. This includes encouraging constructive debates or alternate ideas to solutions.

How to Analyze Critical Data and Information

For every initiative, there is an outcome. That is where analysis comes into play. For a producing leader, it's important to understand the initiatives that are being implemented and then study the outcomes of those strategies and initiatives. To hone in on these results, it's important to not only utilize measurement tools that can put an outcome into perspective for you and your teams, but to also analyze and read into those results to see the meaning behind the analytics. What worked, what didn't, and how something can grow more in future endeavors. Even when it comes to products or services, how did those elements do in the production process or market? How many products were sold? Did a consumer have a good experience with your service? These are questions to be considered regardless of industry because these answers will help to move your organization forward in the future with the next goal.

It's important to not only analyze the success or failure of the initiative, but also to analyze how it correlates back to your overall mission and purpose as an organization. Did it serve the organization to the best of its abilities and if not, could it be done differently to serve the overarching goals of the organization? As a producer, these elements will help create success even if an initiative did not do as well as originally planned.

Marissa Anema (2020), assistant director of marketing and communications at the Rutgers University School of Communication and Information, says,

> Any type of measurement tool [Hootsuite, Google Analytics, Google Ads, etc.] is extremely helpful to building your competency as a producer because it's the only way that's going to measure the work that you're doing towards a goal. For us, it's the number of students that are enrolling. That's the big number that

you want to get to, but before you can look at that as what I'm producing, there's everything else that happens. Having analytical tools to measure the efforts that you're putting in is going to inform the way that you get the bigger results, the end result. It's also keeping your finger on the pulse of the market, so if we see trends changing, then we can start to change our trajectory and change our processes, so that we drive more results and we hopefully reach that goal even more, or maybe even set a new goal because everything that happens leading up to the major goal of production is just as important.

Competency in Action

As it pertains to being a responsible leader, being responsible in the production involves a leader's accountability for the business, teams, and sustainability of the company's operations. Indra Nooyi, former CEO of PepsiCo, embodies many elements of being a successful leader, but puts into perspective how to be a responsible one as well. According to Dool (2019):

> In 12 years as CEO of PepsiCo, Indra Nooyi grew the company's revenues by more than 80 percent, significantly expanded its international footprint, and executed key acquisitions to ensure its future, from Gatorade and Quaker Oats, to Pepsi Bottling and SodaStream. At the same time, she foresaw early key market trends, redirecting the company's focus toward healthier alternatives, including in its soda and snack food offerings, and working to lessen the company's impact on environmentally distressed areas of the world.

Maintaining efficiency, speed, and resourcefulness on a day-to-day basis can be challenging. Some leaders carry out the work as head of a department, but also keep a role in other areas of the department as well. This can help keep them in knowing about the process; however, it can be a juggling act to accomplish. This is where time and project management plays an important role.

According to Kim Guinta, editorial director at Rutgers University Press, in an interview (March 2020),

> Keeping up with everybody else is a challenge, especially when you're trying to do all the other paperwork [of a manager]. I feel like it would be easy to get behind. So time management is important for a producer.

A producer who manages effectively can hold any title within any structure, whether they are the head of an organization or member of a team project. If they are encompassing the following elements, they are producing success in their leadership with their teams. According to Kanaga and Prestridge (2002):

> The Center for Creative Leadership (CCL) has a long history of work with teams. In the course of that work it has become clear that four sets of activities spell the difference between a successful team launch and an unsuccessful one:
>
> 1) Setting purpose and direction
> 2) Defining roles and responsibilities
> 3) Designing procedures and practices
> 4) Building cooperation and relationships.
>
> When you take on the responsibility of leading a team, you can launch your team toward success by addressing all of these elements.

Being a good manager is also about staying positive and encouraging team members. According to Kim Guinta (2020):

> At my other job we had really high targets, and the company didn't run if the people didn't meet their targets. ... The thing I learned is you can only push somebody so far. And if there are no incentives in place, then there is no reason for someone to try extra hard to do something. Fear only motivates you so far.

Another facet of management includes good communication with team members. The most important thing to remember when communicating about work is to be as unambiguous as possible with expectations. This way, not only is everyone on the same page, but a leader is more likely to get the outcome they are expecting.

Martha and Boehm (2008) noted,

> It's very actionable – the difference, for example, between telling the sales force they need to increase revenues by 10 percent (an outcome) and telling them they each need to make two hundred additional sales calls (an action). Good direction also makes the tough decisions between priorities, as opposed to putting them all on an equal footing and making employees decide, when they come to an unavoidable conflict, which is more important. ... so they make the right decisions when they have to.

By being analytical of critical data and information, Jeffrey Bezos has also shown the results of his impactful leadership. Dool (2019) notes:

> For any company, experimentation breeds innovation, and it sets a stale business apart from an obvious leader in the industry. Bezos encourages Amazon employees to experiment constantly, and tests promising ideas with the knowledge that they might fail.

As a leader, to be involved in the process is to provide freedom to your teams, instilling check-in meetings throughout. This can not only help to stay active in your producing role, but also ensure that work is being implemented in the best ways and if a team or member of a team is struggling, to provide more guidance to help the process continue to move. Having that overarching goal, whether a strategy or initiative, helps to keep the focus on the outcome, which is what everyone on the team is working toward. Anema (2020) adds:

> It's definitely a balance between not assuming that the work is getting done and just turning your blind eye to it and then realizing that there's some sort of piece missing, and balancing that with

not constantly checking in with your team and making them feel like the only thing that they're doing is reporting.

Summary

To bring everything together, a leader as producer is a leader who executes on goals and objectives, drives tangible results, and utilizes feedback and experience to inform decisions about the process of reaching these objectives.

It's also important to remember that this guidance is not only meant for those at the top of an organization's structure. Anyone can take this advice into consideration and implement it into their own leadership styles, whether you are an executive, team leader, or team member. Behn (2014) describes how anyone can embody a leader by taking this initiative to drive and produce results within your organization:

> These people are real leaders. They might be the people at the top of the organization's formal hierarchy—those traditionally charged with these responsibilities. But their formal status does not make them leaders. It only gives them the opportunity to exercise leadership. They are not, however, the only ones. If a governor does not want to take on these leadership responsibilities, a department head can. If a cabinet secretary avoids them, an agency director can take them up. Others—people with a purpose—can simply take up the responsibility for producing results. In the process, they exercise leadership.

Being a producer is crucial as producing sustainable results defines the success of the organization. Leaders not only create a compelling vision for the organization, but also drive the implementation and execution to the expected outcomes. They are present for their teams and create the supportive atmosphere that team members feel passionate about the work they do. Similarly, to being a "leader as exemplar," a leader will set the tone in which their teams will work. If a leader does not motivate their teams to produce, the initiatives will not be successfully implemented. If a leader effectively communicates the overall vision and goals of the organization, they will engage employees and will help them feel valued in their roles. They will come to work every day feeling passionate about what they do, which will lead to successful implementation and execution. Furthermore, as a leader as producer, it's important to know how to balance micro- and macro-managing your teams to ensure you are giving them the freedom to get the work done, but also providing the support they may need throughout short- and long-term processes.

Key Takeaways

- Ideas are key, but actions are fundamental: Ideas are ineffective without execution. As leaders, it's crucial to work with your organization, build teams, and bring ideas to fruition that tie back to the organization's vision, purpose, and values.
- It's all about balance: Being involved with your team and taking active measures in the process, but also giving your team the freedom to produce as well without constant interference.
- You're only as strong as your teams: Be there for your teams and utilize their feedback and ideas, not just on the work, but also on your own leadership and ideas. A leader not only produces results on goals and initiatives, but produces opportunities for others to lead and be their own producers.
- There is room for growth in every initiative: Regardless of the work being done, there are always opportunities to grow and see what worked, what didn't, and what could be done differently in the future to achieve better results.

References

Anema, M. March 2020. Personal Communication.

Behn, R. 2014. *The PerformanceStat Potential—A Leadership Strategy for Producing Results*. Brookings Institution Press.

Dool, R. 2019. *12 Months of Leadership Insights: A Compendium of Leadership Lessons from 40 Leaders*. Seattle, WA: Kindle Direct Publishing.

Guinta, K. March 5, 2020. Personal Communication.

Kanaga, K., and S. Prestridge. 2002. *How to Launch a Team Start Right for Success*. Greensboro, NC: Center for Creative Leadership.

Langway, Z. March 2020. Personal Communication.

Martha, B., and M. Boehm. 2008. *Beyond the Babble: Leadership Communication that Drives Results*. 1st ed. San Francisco, CA: Jossey-Bass.

Prior, L. 2020. "Producer/Manager/Leader: The New Leadership Paradigm," *Prior Consulting*. https://www.priorconsulting.com/resources/articles/producer-manager-leader/, (accessed April 24, 2020).

CHAPTER 12

Bringing It All Together

This book is the result of a long journey of exploring the various competencies needed to effectively lead in the twenty-first century. It started 8 years ago with the work GE was doing in China on middle management development and then evolved as GE assessed its overall set of needed global leadership competencies. I used my experiences at GE as the foundation of my notion of Leaderocity^{TM}. As noted earlier, we are not suggesting this is THE list of needed competencies. Our list of the 10 competencies is the result of our research, experiences, and the 30 leader interviews we conducted. It is our suggested list, I am sure there is an argument for adding more, replacing some, or even combining in some form.

We are in an unprecedented time for leaders with heightened scrutiny, fast pacing, a chaotic environment, and the raging war for talent. There is a lot expected of leaders today and they have to perform at speed and out in the open. They have to seamlessly navigate both the strategic and tactical dimensions of their roles and balance the need to be steadfast with adaptability.

Leader tenures are declining. Systemic impatience abounds and often is short-term focused. The best leaders create a compelling vision, communicate it to create broad and deep buy-in, and then lead the execution to the expected results. They do this while navigating the demands for "now" and the strategic longer view. They not only produce results, they also create and embed effective processes for sustainable success. They put in place oversight mechanisms and effectively use them to know when to intervene and when to step back.

Leaders today have to be consummate communicators, effectively engaging a wide range of internal and external stakeholders. The have to be effective in all three main modalities of communication: one-to-one,

one-to-many, and the various "eForms." They have to be effective in creating connections and be able to drive buy-in across and down an organization.

They need courage of conviction to go first and be out-front as the "face" of the organization. They understand the scrutiny and the need to be an exemplar. They have to be consistent in values, attitude, words, actions, and behaviors. They understand there are no private moments, someone is always watching and judging. They have to be able to communicate "purpose" and to live that purpose.

Leaders today also have to embrace "difference" and be able to leverage it as an organizational asset. They are inclusionists who intentionally seek out the various perspectives, insights, and experiences that come with diversity. They do not accept past practices of managing, mitigating, or accepting diversity as a compliance measure. They embrace, celebrate, and leverage diversity for the sustained competitive advantages it can drive. They see the higher social good and purpose as well as the operational value.

Change is not likely to slow down in our working lifetimes. Leaders must be effective change agents. In leading change, they have a dual role. They need to be a source of urgency, discomfort, and energy to break up inertia and to ensure their organizations are change ready. They embed adaptability into the organization's DNA and make change a natural part of the organizational culture. They also need to be the source of psychological comfort—"we can do this." They understand that change does not often come naturally to an organization and it requires persistent and consistent leadership presence and intervention.

Leaders also must deeply understand the value of talent and the need for strategic human capital investments. They know that attracting, recruiting, developing, and retaining the most talent is a critical organization process. They spend much of their time on talent management and development with the intent of creating a vibrant and engaged workforce. They recognize the need to be constantly searching for talent and the global war for talent demands that they find talent not only in nontraditional sources, but also in nontraditional "packages." They actively focus on practices that will positively drive engagement, organizational identity, and commitment.

It is reasonable for any one leader to be equally adept at each of these 10 competencies? Probably not, but the reality of today's macro-environment demands a level of competency in each of them. How much of each is largely situational and contextual, so there is no one right formula. Some will emerge as most critical at various stages of organization life cycles and others may be less needed at certain points. However, it is very likely all 10 will come into play at some point and often may be needed in various blended ways. A key for any leader is to have good triage and diagnostic skills to interpret a situation and authentically adapt the needed competencies.

The best leaders also have a reasonably accurate self-assessment. They confront their own competencies through assessments, self-reflection, and feedback. They seek out what they need to hear versus want to hear. They invest in their own development and surround themselves with others who may compliment their competencies. They seek feedback, listen, reflect, and adapt as needed. They also are not hesitant to delegate and empower the talent they have placed around them.

We offer these competencies to inspire thought, reflection, and debate. We strongly believe leaders need to be life-long learners, constantly challenging their own leadership assumptions, practices, and behaviors. We hope this book offers a chance for both current and aspiring leaders to assess their own competencies and to enhance their leadership practices.

References

Ancona, D. n.d. "Leadership in an Age of Uncertainty." https://thesystemsthinker .com/leadership-in-an-age-of-uncertainty/, (accessed March 19, 2020).

Axon, L., E. Friedman, and K. Jordan. 2015. *Leading Now: Critical Capabilities for a Complex World*. Boston, MA: Harvard Business Publishing Corporate Learning.

Axtell, C., T. Wall, C. Stride, and C. Pepper. 2002. "Familiarity Breeds Content: The Impact of Exposure to Change on Employee Openness and Well Being." *The Journal of Occupational & Organizational Psychology* 75, no. 2, pp. 217-31.

Botelho, E., and S. Kos. 2020. "Unexpected Companies Produce Some of the Best CEOs." https://hbr.org/2020/01/unexpected-companies-produce-some-of-the-best-ceos, (accessed March 17, 2020).

Cisco. 2020. "Transitioning to Workforce 2020." https://www.cisco.com/c/dam/ en_us/training-events/employer_resources/pdfs/Workforce_2020_White_ Paper.pdf, (accessed March 21, 2020).

Erickson, T. 2010. "The Leaders We Need Now." *Harvard Business Review*, May 2010.

Greenspan, A. 2007. *The Age of Turbulence*. New York, NY: Penguin Books.

HP. 2004. "The Adaptive Enterprise." http://whp-aus1.cold.extweb.hp.com/ pub/services/aes/info/ae_59823185en.pdf.

Kaiser, R. 2020. "The Best Leaders Are Versatile Ones." https://hbr.org/2020/03/ the-best-leaders-are-versatile-ones, (accessed March 18, 2020).

Kotler, P., and J. Caslione. 2009. *Chaotics: The Business of Managing and Marketing in the Age of Turbulence*. New York, NY: Amacom.

Lombardi, D. 1997. *Reorganization and Renewal: Strategies for Healthcare Leaders*. Chicago, IL: American College of Healthcare Executives.

Manciagli, D. 2016. "4 Biggest Challenges Facing Business Leaders Today." https:// www.bizjournals.com/bizjournals/how-to/growth-strategies/2016/04/4-biggest-challenges-facing-business-leaders-today.html, (accessed March 20, 2020).

Morieux, Y., and P. Tollman. 2014. *Six Simple Rules: How to Manage Complexity without Getting Complicated*. Boston, MA: Harvard Business Review Press.

Nicholls, J. 2017. "Inside Crotonville: GE's Corporate Vault Unlocked." https:// www.ge.com/reports/inside-crotonville-ges-corporate-vault-unlocked/, (accessed March 17, 2020).

Poscente, V. 2008. *The Age of Speed*. New York, NY: Ballantine Books.

Quality Digest. n.d. "Conversations with Stephen Covey, Tom Peters and Peter Senge." https://www.qualitydigest.com/nov96/conversa.html, (accessed March 19, 2020).

Raia, M. 2018. "How to Lead through Crisis." https://www.integrify.com/blog/posts/how-to-lead-through-chaos/, (accessed March 19, 2020).

Russell Reynolds Associates. 2016. "Leadership through Uncertainty: 10 Enduring Lessons for Turbulent Times." https://www.russellreynolds.com/en/Insights/thought-leadership/Documents/R60707-rr-0080-Leadership%20under%20Uncertainty%20v2.pdf, (accessed March 19, 2020).

Stevenson, S. 2014. "How Do You Make Better Managers." https://slate.com/business/2014/06/ges-crotonville-management-campus-where-future-company-leaders-are-trained.html, (accessed March 17, 2020).

Tulgan, B. 2000. *Just in Time Leadership*. Boston, MA: HRD Press.

U.S. Army Heritage and Education Center. July 10, 2018. "Who First Originated the Term VUCA (Volatility, Uncertainty, Complexity and Ambiguity)?" USAHEC Ask Us a Question. The United States Army War College.

Vaill, P.B. 1996. *Learning as a Way of Being: Strategies for Survival in a World of Permanent White Water*. The Jossey-Bass Business and Management Series. San Francisco, CA: Jossey-Bass.

Voepel, S. 2003. *The Mobile Company, an Advanced Organizational Model for Mobilizing Knowledge Innovation and Value Creation*. St. Gallen, Switzerland: IFPM.

Volini, E., J. Schwartz, I. Roy, M. Hauptmann, Y. Van Durme, B. Denny, and J. Bersin. 2019. "Leadership for the 21st Century: The Intersection of the Traditional and the New," *Deloitte Insights*. https://www2.deloitte.com/us/en/insights/focus/human-capital-trends/2019/21st-century-leadership-challenges-and-development.html#, (accessed March 20, 2020).

White, C. 2006. *Seismic Shifts: Leading in Times of Change*. Toronto, Canada: United Church Publishing House.

About the Author

Dr. Richard Dool is currently the Managing Director of Leaderocity^{TM}, LLC, a management consultancy offering solutions for change management, strategic development, leadership communication and organizational renewal.

Dr. Dool is on the faculty at Rutgers University School of Communication and Information where he is also the Director of the Masters in Communication and Media program and the Masters in Health Communication and Information.

Dr. Dool has a MA in Strategic Communication and Leadership, a MS in Management and a Doctorate in Management/Organizational Processes. Dr. Dool is an active author, researcher and presenter in these areas. He is the author of "Enervative Change: The Impact of Persistent Change Initiatives on Job Satisfaction. He has also published: "How Generation Z Wants to be Led" and "12 Months of Leadership Insights: A Compendium of Leadership Lessons from 40 Leaders."

Dr. Dool is a Fellow of the Institute of Leadership and Management (UK) and on the Board of Advisors of the International Academy of Management and Business.

Dr. Dool has a comprehensive and diverse executive level leadership background including leading an $800M division of AT&T, global leadership roles (GE), and serving 12 years as CEO of both public and private companies. Background includes rescuing a company from near bankruptcy, leading the acquisition or divestiture of 11 companies and effectively managing companies in the US, UK, China, Brazil, Germany, France, India and Australia. He has significant operational experience in executive leadership, general management, sales/commercial leadership, product management, project management and marketing leadership positions. Successful leadership experience in a variety of settings including multi-national, multicultural and virtual environments. He has been on the Board of Directors of five different companies as well as a member of several Boards of Advisors.

Dr. Dool comes from a US Marine family and served in the Marines as well.

Index

OTHER TITLES IN THE HUMAN RESOURCE MANAGEMENT AND ORGANIZATIONAL BEHAVIOR COLLECTION

Concise and Applied Business Books

The Collection listed above is one of 30 business subject collections that Business Expert Press has grown to make BEP a premiere publisher of print and digital books. Our concise and applied books are for…

- Professionals and Practitioners
- Faculty who adopt our books for courses
- Librarians who know that BEP's Digital Libraries are a unique way to offer students ebooks to download, not restricted with any digital rights management
- Executive Training Course Leaders
- Business Seminar Organizers

Business Expert Press books are for anyone who needs to dig deeper on business ideas, goals, and solutions to everyday problems. Whether one print book, one ebook, or buying a digital library of 110 ebooks, we remain the affordable and smart way to be business smart. For more information, please visit **www.businessexpertpress.com**, or contact **sales@businessexpertpress.com**.

www.ingramcontent.com/pod-product-compliance
Lightning Source LLC
Chambersburg PA
CBHW050459190326
41458CB00005B/1357